The Catholic
Avant-Garde

The Catholic Avant-Garde

French Catholicism Since World War II

Jean-Marie Domenach and Robert de Montvalon

 New York   Chicago   San Francisco
Holt, Rinehart and Winston

BX1530.2

D613

Translated from the French by Brigid Elson,
Jacqueline Pace, Irene Uribe, and Frances Wilms.

Designer: Ernst Reichl
81890-0117
Printed in the United States of America

Acknowledgments

Grateful acknowledgment is made to the following publishers who have so generously granted permission to reprint from their publications:

Aubier, Paris, for passages from *Le sens de l'existence selon saint Jean de la Croix*, by G. Morel, S.J. (1961).
Blackfriars, London, for passages from *Revolution in a City Parish*, by G. Michonneau (1951).
Bonne Press (Editions de la), Paris, for passages from *Carnets spirituels*, by Emmanuel Cardinal Suhard (1952).
Bulletin du cercle saint Jean Baptiste for excerpts from "Rencontre des religions et rencontre des personnes," by P. A. Lesort, No. 24 (1963).
Cerf (Les Éditions du), Paris, for excerpts from the following books and periodicals: *Problèmes missionaires de la France rurale*, by Fernand Boulard (1949); Father Bouyer in *La Maison-Dieu*, No. 31; *La Maison-Dieu*, "Anthropologie et Liturgie," by M. D. Chenu, O.P., No. 12 (1947); *La vie intellectuelle*, "Le sacerdoce des prêtres-ouvriers," by M. D. Chenu, O.P. (February, 1954); *Vraie et fausse reforme dans l'Eglise*, by Yves Congar (1950); *Se garder libre, journal 1947–1954*, by M. A. Couturier, O.P. (1961); *Civilisation de l'atome*, by Dominique Dubarle, O.P. (1962); *La vie intellectuelle*, "L'expérience du MRP," by Joseph Hours (May, 1948); *La vie intellectuelle*, "A propos des chrétiens progressistes," by A. J. Maydieu and A. Z. Serrand (March, 1949); *Pas de vie chrétienne sans communauté*, by G. Michonneau (1960); *Redécouverte du Jeune*, by P. R. Régamey, O.P. et al. (1959); and for the statement by the editors of *La Quinzaine* in *La vie intellectuelle* (March, 1949).
Chronique Sociale de France, Paris, for excerpts from "L'Eglise de France en état de concile," by Robert de Montvalon, No. 3–4 (June 15, 1962).
Cross Currents, New York, for excerpts from "Christian Faith and Civilization," by Emmanuel Mounier (Fall, 1950), and from "Christianity and Laicity," by Joseph Vialatoux and André Latreille (Winter, 1952).
L'Express, Paris, for excerpts from "The Attitude of Catholics Towards the Elections," by François Mauriac (December 8, 1955); from "Interference," by François Mauriac (December 22, 1955); and from "Bloc-Notes," by François Mauriac (May 7, 1954).

v

Fides Publishers, Inc., Notre Dame, Indiana, for passages from *Priests Among Men*, by Emmanuel Cardinal Suhard (1951).

Gallimard (Editions), Paris, for passages from *L'Affaire Henri Martin*, by J. M. Domenach.

Harper & Row, Publishers, Inc., New York, for passages from *The Divine Milieu* by Pierre Teilhard de Chardin (English translation copyright 1960 by Wm. Collins Sons & Co., London, and Harper & Brothers, New York; originally published in French as *Le Milieu Divin*, copyright 1957 by Editions du Seuil, Paris); and for passages from *The Phenomenon of Man* by Pierre Teilhard de Chardin (copyright 1955 by Editions du Seuil, Paris; copyright © 1959 in the English translation by Wm. Collins Sons & Co., Ltd., London, and Harper & Row, Publishers, New York).

Helicon Press, Inc., Baltimore, Maryland, and Darton, Longman & Todd Ltd., London, for excerpts from *Brothers of Men*, by René Voillaume.

Herder & Herder, Inc., New York, for excerpts from *Religious Art in the Twentieth Century*, by P. R. Régamey, O.P. (1963); and from *Non-Violence and the Christian Conscience*, by P. R. Régamey, O.P. (1966).

Holt, Rinehart and Winston, Inc., New York, for passages from *Priest and Worker*, by Henri Perrin, translated by Bernard Wall. Copyright © 1958 by Editions du Seuil. Copyright © 1964 by Holt, Rinehart and Winston, Inc.

Horay et Cie, Paris, for excerpts from "Notre civilisation, est-elle malade?" in *Semaine des intellectuels catholiques, 1960*, by François Perroux (1961).

Ouvrières (Editions), Paris, for passages from *Suicide ou survie de l'Occident?* by L. J. Lebret, O.P. (1958).

Routledge & Kegan Paul Ltd., London, for passages from *The Worker-Priests, A Collective Documentation*, translated by John Petrie (1956).

Sheed & Ward, Inc., New York, and Burns & Oates Ltd., London, for passages from *Catholicism: A Study of Dogma in Relation to the Corporate Destiny of Mankind*, by Henri de Lubac, S.J. (1958).

Seuil (Editions du), Paris, for passages from *Les evénements et la foi*, by M. I. Montuclard (1951); from *Feu la chrétienté*, by Emmanuel Mounier (1951); from *Contre la torture*, by Pierre-Henri Simon (1957); and from *Les chrétiens dans le monde rural*, by P. Toulat, A. Bougeard, and J. Templier (1964).

Sheed & Ward, Inc., New York, and Sheed & Ward Ltd., London, for passages from *France Pagan?*, by Maisie Ward, copyright 1949 by Sheed & Ward, Inc., New York.

Contents

Introduction　3

I Christianity and the Modern World

Religious Renewal and Contemporary Values　6
Henri de Lubac
M. I. Montuclard
The Example of Teilhard　14
Pierre Teilhard de Chardin
Emmanuel Mounier
M. I. Montuclard
Yves Congar
The Testimony of Abbé Depierre　26
André Depierre

II A Mission Country

Facing Facts　48
Henri Godin
Emmanuel Cardinal Suhard
Henri Perrin
A Missionary Church　54
Emmanuel Cardinal Suhard
Mission de France
Les chrétiens dans le monde rural
The Priest-Worker Experiment　61
Henri Perrin
Jean Lacroix
M. I. Montuclard
Condemnation and Reactions　73

Letter of Thirty-One Priest-Workers
to Cardinal Feltin
M. D. Chenu
François Perroux

III Toward a Christian Realism

Immanence and Transcendence   89
Maurice Blondel
Yves de Montcheuil
Internal Controversy   92
Alain Barrère
André Vial
Doctrinal Note on the ACJF
Route Statement
Henri Marrou
Universal Science and an Economy for Man   101
Dominique Dubarle
François Perroux
The Lesson of Emmaüs   105
Abbé Pierre

IV The Church Apostolic

Liturgy and Religious Education   109
G. Michonneau
M. D. Chenu
The Renewal of Religious Art   118
M. A. Couturier
P. R. Régamey
Toward a Contemporary Spirituality   122
René Voillaume
P. R. Régamey
G. Morel
Robert de Montvalon

V The Secular City

The School Question   130
  Henri Marrou
  Jacques Natanson
The Church and Civil Society   135
  Emmanuel Mounier
  Joseph Vialatoux and André Latreille
  Cardinal Gerlier
Pluralism in Politics   143
  Joseph Hours
  François Mauriac
  Abbé Boulier
  Emmanuel Mounier
  M. I. Montuclard
  Jean-Marie Domenach
Christianity and Socialism   155
  Jean-Marie Domenach
  Henri Bartoli
  André Mandouze
  A. J. Maydieu
  Paul Fraisse
  La Quinzaine
  Jean Lacroix
The Development of Christian
  Trade-Unionism   173
  C. Savouillan
Changes in Rural Life   179
  Fernand Boulard
  P. Toulat, A. Bougeard, and J. Templier

VI The Struggle Against Colonialism

The Beginnings of Protest   184
  Jean-Marie Domenach

François Mauriac
Louis Massignon
The Algerian War   189
Henri Marrou
Pierre-Henri Simon
The Witness of Priests   192
Abbé Bérenguer
Abbé Carteron
The Scandal of Conscience   199
Jean Le Meur
Jo Pyronnet

VII   World Violence and World Peace

Is Christianity Western?   210
Robert de Montvalon
Declaration of the Bishops of West
Africa and Togo
L. J. Lebret
Blessed Are the Peacemakers   217
Archbishop H. Chappoulie
P. R. Régamey
Emmanuel Mounier
The Brotherhood of Man   226
Jean Frisque
Paul André Lesort

Conclusion: A New Christianity   231

Notes   241

The Catholic
Avant-Garde

Introduction

THIS book is not an attempt to recount history or to hand out prizes. It is a collection of testimony and key documents dealing with the great renewal which has shaken French Catholicism since World War II.

We have not mentioned every important or decisive figure: this would have meant writing an encyclopedia. Nor have we tried to draw up a complete balance sheet. Instead, we have tried to acquaint the reader with some of the actors in an impassioned and meaningful part of history.

Some of them will be familiar names, at least to those who know something of French Catholicism—famous writers, spiritual leaders, theologians, and the priest-workers; others are more obscure. As a group they may seem both attractive and irritating. These sons of the "eldest daughter of the Church" often flaunt a claim, in spite of themselves, to be model Christians and prophets. But we French are neither universal doctors nor incendiaries. We do not represent the whole world; we are not the Church. We do, however, have a certain virile habit of faith. Although tradition floods our memory, we have never completely forgotten that it is inventive, as the texts which follow will demonstrate. Those who praise French Catholics, as well as those who complain about them, will discover that they are faithful Christians who continue to search.

Perhaps our chief merit is a natural sensitivity to the great changes which have marked the twentieth century since the beginning of the First World War. It is something for which we deserve no credit. We live between the ocean and the rest of the continent, between north and south. Problems strike us full in the face, like spray from the sea. Our very location forces us into the role of troublemaker, the picador who goads the bull, the child who asks "Why?" We are not amazing Christians; we are simply Christians who are amazed.

More precisely, we include in our ranks many Christians who dare to be amazed. Naturally, there are others who swear that the seekers are going to lose both themselves and their faith. From there it is but one step to thinking that French Catholicism is teetering on the border of heresy and schism. The step seems easy when intramural polemics are played out in headlines, but the real situation is quite different.

In trying to choose texts without drawing up a kind of inventory, we had to make rules for our selection. Should we include Catholic liberals and ignore conservatives? These categories are too political to be satisfactory. It is true that some French Catholics have been carrying on a rear-guard battle against the modern world since 1789. But is this obstinacy a form of faith or a defect of character? Such an attitude is held only by a small minority, who are paralyzed by passion; they are hardly representative of French Catholicism.

In preparing this book it became clear that the history of the Church in France during the last twenty years is not that of a merciless struggle between progressives and reactionaries but the history of a believing people which has set out en route. The internal quarrels are not over (they never will be), but all have been carried forward, in the direction, we can now see, of the Council. It would be foolish to say that the Council was simply reaping the harvest of the Church of France. Nevertheless, our experiments, along with those of other countries, were central to the work of the Council.

A movement which was born more than a century ago, and was checked by the Revolution of 1848, sowed the seeds of ideas put forward by a bitter Lamennais and an ardent Lacordaire, and, after many detours and disappointments, culminated in the Council. It is a truly Christian movement, despite its errors and the unworthiness of its participants. It has not been the action of a sect but of a people; not a political struggle waged by spiritual leaders, but the movement of believers who wanted to be true neighbors and loyal sons of the living God. The texts we cite show that the Christian renaissance in France involves both praise of God and brotherly service, contemplation and action, responsibility for present time and hope in the end of time—which is also the ultimate renaissance.

If this book is biased, therefore, at least it is not sectarian. The reader should not look for the war songs of one group of Christians which wants to triumph over others, but for a story of faith advancing through history.

JEAN-MARIE DOMENACH
ROBERT DE MONTVALON

August 1966

1

Christianity and the Modern World

Religious Renewal and Contemporary Values

The defeat of the French Army and the Occupation of
1940 caused a trauma that was more than political. It
became the occasion for an examination of conscience;
many Frenchmen began to reflect on their personal and
collective destinies. The catastrophe which overthrew the
national structure shook all certitudes and led men to question themselves on their religion. Was the Church more
solid than the Republic which had just collapsed? Were
spiritual defeats not worse than those of institutions and
leaders?

Defeat and humiliation also led to hope; men naturally
turned back to essentials, to find reasons for living and
dying. The Catholic renewal was suddenly to take on larger
dimensions. In the ordeal, there began a re-examination of

every aspect of Catholicism, to rediscover the foundation of the Church.

In 1941 Father de Lubac, one of the theologians who had prepared this renewal, traced its principal line of development. After mentioning some of its intellectual origins, he exclaimed:

But why speak of books and schools? For what gives ground for the greatest confidence is that this is no mere surface agitation, that the theologians themselves, the interpreters of the living tradition, are urged forward by a revival which is reflected primarily in events because it springs from the very depths of the Catholic conscience. Take, for example, the success from a religious point of view of such authors as Péguy or Claudel. Is it not extremely significant? But principally we should realize all the doctrinal implications of those great movements which in our day show so plainly the vitality of the Church: the missionary movement, the liturgical movement—so very different from that archaeological sectarian spirit that at one time merely kept it in check—social movements like the JOC in Belgium or in France. But we realize, too, the need in which they stand, if they are to fulfill their promise, of fully enlightened support and guidance. Again we see the urgent necessity of strictly theological doctrinal elaboration.

Just to imitate primitive Christianity of the Middle Ages will not be enough. We can revive the Fathers' all-embracing humanism and recover the spirit of their mystical exegesis only by an assimilation which is at the same time a transformation. For although the Church rests on eternal foundations, it is in a continual state of rebuilding, and since the Fathers' time it has undergone many changes in style; and without in any way considering ourselves better than our Fathers, what we in turn have to build for our own use must be built in our own style, that is, one that is adapted to our own needs and problems. We should gain nothing at all by breaking with an unhealthy individualism if in its place we dreamt of an impossible return to the past, for that is either an illusion which breeds schisms or a childish fancy which dulls the mind. Two conditions must govern our contemplation of the past. We must recognize, in the first place, the great diversity of the theories which have been professed in the course of Christian history on those innumerable subjects where religious truth comes in contact with our human preoccupations. Secondly, we must realize to how great an extent these theories depend on social, intellectual, or cultural conditions in a state of constant development. Only so can we contemplate and admire in all security the imposing unity of the great current of tradition, bearing in its ever changing waves, free from all contamination, the same indefectible belief. It is only when we have realized very keenly how different we necessarily are in our human reactions, even toward revelation, and in our human methods of thought, even about dogma —from St. Paul or Origen, St. Thomas Aquinas or Bossuet, a monk of the Thebaid, a medieval craftsman, or a Chinese neophyte—that we shall be conscious of the full intimacy of our profound union with them all in this same dogma by which they lived as we live today: in eadem doctrina eademque sententia. Then a return to the sources of antiquity will be the very opposite of an escape into a dead past. We shall understand how disastrous it would be if we were to forgo the great heritage which comes to us from the centuries of analysis and scientific research, as well as from the definitive results, the clarifications which emerge from the controversies. We shall not condemn self-examination or spiritual experience as if they derived from a merely individualist psychology or narcissist introspection, any more than, by an analogous method of misinterpretation, we shall confuse transcendental speculation with an abstract discarnate idealism. Even in our criticism of individualism we shall recognize that much of human progress has been bound up with its expansion, and that it is a question not so much of repudiating it as of rising above it. So, too, shall we reject the notion that the modern age has experienced outside the Church only error and decadence. That is an illusion, a temptation to which we have yielded only too often. The epoch of a "separated" philosophy was providential, like all others, and the fruits of the immense effort of thought which was undertaken in its name, and is still being undertaken, ought not, through our fault, to be left outside Catholicism. Certainly it requires a far more generous perspicacity to give a favorable reception to what has arisen outside our own body than to gather up what had at one time flourished within it and give it new life.

A much keener discernment, too, is necessary if mistakes are to be avoided. So the work that is called for at the present day is in many respects far more delicate than that required in the patristic age, in St. Thomas Aquinas' time or even in the "humanist" epoch. It demands a comprehensive combination of opposing qualities, each of them brought to a high degree of excellence, one buttressed, so to say, on another, and braced with the greatest tension. Who would not feel overwhelmed and disheartened at the very outset in face of such requirements, however unassuming the part which he hopes to play in the great common task? But once again it is faith that wins the victory, and he who realizes his helplessness retires within himself and with the whole Church begs for the grace of the Holy Spirit.[1]

At the same time, at Lyons, a Dominican, Father M. I. Montuclard, surrounded himself with a small intellectual brotherhood whose self-imposed task was to emphasize the community aspect of the Church and to seek a way for Christians to involve themselves actively in the new society which would emerge from the war. The title of the group was significant: *Jeunesse de l'Eglise.** Instead of setting Catholic dogma and contemporary impiety in opposition, Father Montuclard proclaimed the existence of modern values which are no less authentic for often asserting themselves against faith:

The trends of the time seem to have two correlative but distinct elements: doctrinal systems, and psychosociological forces which contain their living reality. To give only one example: Marxist philosophy and Communist aspiration. Doctrines reinforce aspirations; they lead them toward clarity, give them a legitimacy, reveal their possibilities, and teach them how to achieve their purposes. But psychosociological forces usually burst out first; they are spontaneous reactions of the human conscience to the needs and circumstances of the times. Systems are elaborated afterward, and are only episodic manifestations, schematic and impoverished, of a deep and enduring current. Marx, Proudhon, Juarès, and Lenin represent the successive and varying moments of conscience in the historical unfolding of proletarian aspiration. They are not identical with it, any more than Descartes is with the Encyclopedia, or Hegel, Valéry, and Brunschwig are with the

* When France was liberated, the community settled in the outskirts of Paris. In addition to the irregularly published journal, *Jeunesse de l'Eglise*, Father Montuclard also brought out *Lettres aux Impatients* and a book dealing with the main ideas of the movement, *Les evénements et la foi* (ed. du Seuil). After the condemnation of these ideas in October 1953, the community was dissolved.

rationalist aspiration. The appreciation of these great humanistic currents of our time will vary considerably, depending on whether one is looking for doctrinal truth or the value of their tendencies. . . .

An observer with even the least perception can see that the contemporary conscience is constituted and directed by a certain number of half-intellectual, half-affective ideals and postulates. These obviously include liberty, justice, tolerance, democracy, solidarity and a sense of the collective, love (as a spiritual élan incarnated in sex), sincerity, experimental evidence (as the criterion of evidence and method of thinking), progress (that is, a preference for what is new and spontaneous over what is old and fixed), the sense of the grandeur and development of the world and humanity. . . .

The Christian will immediately see that these ideals and postulates are so exactly based on the necessities of the moment that without the dynamism which they arouse, man and society would be condemned to spiritual decline. These ideals and postulates have not been chosen arbitrarily. They are not the idols of aesthetes or the fantasies of dreamers. No one has superimposed them on the modern conscience; they emerged of themselves out of an instinctive reaction to the deficiencies of our society. . . .

Modern man is surely neither more foolish nor wiser than his predecessors. But he has become more aware of his dignity and autonomy and is determined that they be respected. He has little patience with unjustified privilege, or discipline imposed by an authority whose decisions he had no part in. The conservatism of orthodoxy; lies which inevitably favor an exterior, meddling morality; and the hypocrisy of formal marriages, in which neither love nor fidelity is present have alienated him from the Church. That is why he struggles so energetically for institutions and a style of life which allow for human growth. He also sees the absurdity of individualism in a world which progress is making more interdependent every day. Moreover, since this world is divided by rival opinions, where will he find the cement of its unity, if not in a respect for all convictions, so long as they do not undermine some fundamental necessity of life in common? On the other hand, faced with a universe whose dimensions and resources must be measured anew each day, will man fail to spiritualize in some way, in a grand and hopeful vision, these unlimited forces which he must master?

In short, these ideals and postulates are the most recent steps of the human spirit along the road of its own development. Because men are convinced of the necessity of this development, they prefer, despite everything, the excesses of today to those which the memory of past civilization has left us. The abuses of authority, of social constraint, of abstract dialectic, of absolutism in the realm of opinion and of property . . . would strike at contemporary man's most essential reasons for living, hoping, and remaining faithful to a high idea of himself; they would destroy him spiritually. If present society, despite the gigantic oppression of the material forces used by human industry, has not quite lost its soul, this is due in part to the appearance of these new values.[2]

But these new values remain for the most part foreign to Christianity, which is weighed down by values and attitudes formed in the past:

The Christian world today as a whole is extremely sensitive to values which in themselves are complementary, but historically are in opposition to those of contemporary society.

In the majority of cases, even after we recognize that words and attitudes sometimes say one thing and mean another, is it debatable that the Christian world is more responsive to authority than liberty, to guarantees of order than to the necessary demands of justice, to government by one man than to political democracy, to tradition than to progress? . . .

It is on points like these that the modern world and the Christian world oppose each other. The Christian world affirms a table of values which, apart from some adaptations, remains one made necessary by yesterday's social structures and mentality. The modern world, in order to respond to different historical circumstances, struggles (most often against the Christian world) for a new table on which the values that are inscribed are complementary, and, in terms of today's needs, fundamental.[3]

Writing elsewhere in *Jeunesse de l'Eglise*, Father Sertillanges stated that Christianity should not reject "pagan virtues," but integrate them:

On what point should we concentrate the effort to reform? I would not hesitate to reply paradoxically: on the restoration of the natural virtues. In order to be Christians, it is more than ever necessary to be men. In the conditions which will most likely prevail in the future, the most efficacious charity will be on the side of the greatest truth. There was an outcry recently because I wrote that, in order to have a right to justice, it was first necessary to be just. Such a controversy will be useful if it leads us to be more just! I would like to provoke another helpful disturbance today by saying that charity will have a hold on us only to the extent that we are men. Just as the man of love cannot do without

*the virtues of strength and justice, the religious man cannot
dispense with the natural virtues. . . .*

*In the struggle between paganism and Christianity, the
latter will triumph only if it first integrates pagan virtues.*[4]

The Example of Teilhard

Long before this, Teilhard de Chardin had put forth the
same ideas, but they remained confined to a narrow circle.
The shock of the Occupation opened a wider audience to
them, including the young Christians in the Resistance:*

Teilhard was an eminent scientist who experienced, and
overcame, the conflict between faith and modern values
which paralyzed Christians and kept many others from
faith. He had discovered in evolution the track of God, and
his mystic vision linked living matter with divine spirit. His
motto was "To go to heaven *through* the earth"; this meant
that man, associated with the creative act of God, co-oper-
ated in the fulfillment of the world. At Peking in 1940,
where he was pursuing research in paleontology, he wrote
these pages, which were to become part of *The Phenomenon of Man*:

*To outward appearance, the modern world was born of
an antireligious movement: man becoming self-sufficient
and reason supplanting belief. Our generation and the two
that preceded it have heard little but talk of the conflict
between science and faith; indeed it seemed at one moment
a foregone conclusion that the former was destined to take
the place of the latter.*

---

* His major works began to be published by editions du Seuil only in
1955. Biographical and bibliographical details, including references to
English-language editions, are clarified in Claude Cuénot's biography,
Teilhard de Chardin (Baltimore: Helicon Press, 1965).

But, inasmuch as the tension is prolonged, the conflict visibly seems to need to be resolved in terms of an entirely different form of equilibrium—not in elimination, nor duality, but in synthesis. After close on two centuries of passionate struggles, neither science nor faith has succeeded in discrediting its adversary. On the contrary, it becomes obvious that neither can develop normally without the other. And the reason is simple: the same life animates both. Neither in its impetus nor its achievements can science go to its limits without becoming tinged with mysticism and charged with faith.

Firstly in its impetus. We touched on this point when dealing with the problem of action. Man will only continue to work and to research so long as he is prompted by a passionate interest. Now this interest is entirely dependent on the conviction, strictly undemonstrable to science, that the universe has a direction and that it could—indeed, if we are faithful, it should—result in some sort of irreversible perfection. Hence comes belief in progress.

Secondly in its construction. Scientifically we can envisage an almost indefinite improvement in the human organism and human society. But as soon as we try to put our dreams into practice, we realise that the problem remains indeterminate or even insoluble unless, with some partially super-rational intuition, we admit the convergent properties of the world we belong to. Hence belief in unity.

Furthermore, if we decide, under the pressure of facts, in favour of an optimism of unification, we run into the technical necessity of discovering—in addition to the impetus required to push us forward and in addition to the particular objective which should determine our route—the special binder or cement which will associate our lives together, vitally, without diminishing or distorting them. Hence, belief in a supremely attractive centre which has personality.

*In short, as soon as science outgrows the analytic investi-
gations which constitute its lower and preliminary stages,
and passes on to synthesis—synthesis which naturally culminates in the realisation of some superior state of humanity
—it is at once led to foresee and place its stakes on the
future and on the all. And with that it out-distances itself
and emerges in terms of option and adoration.*

*Thus Renan and the nineteenth century were not wrong
to speak of a Religion of Science. Their mistake was not to
see that their cult of humanity implied the re-integration, in
a renewed form, of those very spiritual forces they claimed
to be getting rid of.*

*When, in the universe in movement to which we have
just awakened, we look at the temporal and spatial series
diverging and amplifying themselves around and behind us
like the laminae of a cone, we are perhaps engaging in pure
science. But when we turn towards the summit, towards the
totality and the future, we cannot help engaging in religion.*

*Religion and science are the two conjugated faces or
phases of one and the same act of complete knowledge—the
only one which can embrace the past and future of evolution so as to contemplate, measure and fulfil them.*

*In the mutual reinforcement of these two still opposed
powers, in the conjunction of reason and mysticism, the
human spirit is destined, by the very nature of its development, to find the uttermost degree of its penetration with
the maximum of its vital force.*[5]

It was this reconciliation that excited Teilhard, since it
presupposed a conversion in the attitudes and language of
the Church. There must be an end to the condemnation of
humanism under the pretext that its pride rises up in opposition to God. Teilhard asks Christians to embrace the

whole world and to be pioneers in the gigantic effort of humanity to become fully conscious and finally to transcend itself:

How could we be deserters, or sceptical about the future of the tangible world? How could we be repelled by human labour? How little you know us! You suspect us of not sharing your concern and your hopes and your exaltation at the penetration of mysteries and the conquest of the forces of nature. "Emotions of this kind," you say, "can only be shared by men struggling side by side for existence; whereas you Christians profess to be saved already." As though for us as for you, indeed far more than for you, it were not a matter of life and death that the earth should flourish to the uttermost of its natural powers. As far as you are concerned (and it is here that you are not yet human enough, you do not go to the limits of your humanity) it is simply a matter of the success or failure of a reality which remains vague and precarious even when conceived in the form of some super-humanity. For us it is a question in a true sense of achieving the victory of no less than a God. One thing is infinitely disappointing, I grant you: far too many Christians are insufficiently conscious of the "divine" responsibilities of their lives, and live like other men, giving only half of themselves, never experiencing the spur or the intoxication of furthering the Kingdom of God in every domain of mankind. But do not blame anything but our weakness: our faith imposes on us the right and the duty to throw ourselves into the things of the earth. As much as you, and even better than you (because, of the two of us, I alone am in a position to prolong the perspectives of my endeavour to infinity, in conformity with the requirements of my present intention) I want to dedicate myself body and soul to the sacred duty of research. We must test every barrier, try every path, plumb every abyss. Nihil intentatum . . . God wills it, who willed that He should have need of it. You are men, you say? Plus et ego.

Plus et ego. There can be no doubt of it. At a time when the consciousness of its own powers and possibilities is legitimately awakening in a mankind now ready to become adult, one of the first apologetic duties of the Christian is to show, by the logic of his religious views and still more by the logic of his action, that the Incarnate God did not come to diminish the magnificent responsibility and splendid ambition that is ours: of becoming our own self. Once again, non minuit, sed sacravit. No, Christianity is not, as it is sometimes presented and sometimes practised, an additional burden of observances and obligations to weigh down and increase the already heavy load, or to multiply the already paralysing ties of social life. It is, in fact, a soul of immense power which bestows significance and beauty and a new lightness on what we are already doing. It is true that it sets us on the road towards unsuspected heights. But the slope which leads to these heights is linked so closely with the one we were already climbing naturally, that there is nothing so distinctively human in the Christian as his detachment.[6]

Since 1932 Esprit had included among its chief goals "breaking the alliance of the Christian world with the established disorder." Its founder, Emmanuel Mounier* agreed readily with Montuclard's assertion that a great many modern values are Christian values:

---

* The chief texts of Emmanuel Mounier dealing with Christianity have been collected in Feu la Chrétienté, in Oeuvres, III; see also L'affrontement chrétien, also in Oeuvres, III, translated as The Spoil of the Violent, Cross Currents, Winter, Spring, Summer, 1961.

The scandal is not that they were born outside the Christian world, because every augmentation of humanity's spiritual patrimony belongs, for the Christian, to the catholicity of the Church. The scandal is that Christendom as a social historical entity did not collaborate in their birth, that they were assimilated badly, and are still little known.

We cannot recall too often that the Christian world, understood sociologically at a given moment in history, is not Christianity, and that it may be giving a very unfaithful expression of Christianity. The Western Christian world today usually behaves according to a practical scale of values whose sociological component, which for a century has been chiefly bourgeois, has taken on such an importance that it usually overshadows the genuine Christian scale of values.

A problem immediately presents itself: if Christians must enter the modern world, if, as Sertillanges demanded, they must retrieve the values which seem to be in opposition to them, how is this reconciliation to be accomplished? Mounier insisted that it was not simply a matter of "being incarnate" in this unfamiliar universe:

The strategy of "incarnation" was worth while as long as a world impregnated by Christianity allowed the Christian message to be spread. Under the new conditions this is no longer possible. A world which has a system of values and structures independent of Christianity—not really antagonistic, merely different from it—obviously refuses to be consecrated by a universe which is foreign to it.

Homage is the first duty of a Christian when confronted with a truth, no matter where it comes from. No one disputes the fact that despite zeal and effort which were more heroic and ardent than well-directed, the Christian world as a whole has often been far behind in the effort to organize the world, which has been going on for two centuries, especially in political, social, and economic areas. In these matters, therefore, a basic moral and intellectual honesty requires the Christian to start learning instead of dogmatizing or hastily making useless inferences. Today he would more often do better to be interested in assuming (and correcting) values which were born historically outside his sociological climate than in "incarnating" his own preconceptions.

Thus, on different levels—this time sociological rather than geographical—Christianity is once again torn between Peter and Paul, between faith in renewal through contact with the Gentiles, and the spiritual protectionism of the primitive community. It is one thing to say that Christianity possesses the unique words of Life, but whether the Christian world today is the only or major bearer of these words, whether the ways of God are necessarily those of Christendom's majority judgments, is quite a different question. Bernanos has detected apostasy among us.* I sense it myself sometimes in the more superficial writings of young Christian Communists. We are not being suffocated by these wild, generous children, however, but by our most orthodox behavior, by distressing experiences at Mass, and the terrible emptiness of so many sermons.

Empty like an empty gourd or an empty cask. These words describe the element within us which accepts and is resigned to everything—not our inner principle of activity and protest.

An error or a heresy can be refuted, condemned, or extirpated. But you do not refute a drama, and Christianity, for all its surface calm, is confronted today with the

* Georges Bernanos had reproached certain young Catholics with letting themselves be drawn out of the Church by Marxist influence. (Eds.)

most fearful drama in its history. Heresy is not the threat; Christianity no longer excites people enough for that. The real menace is a silent apostasy made up of surrounding indifference and its own distraction. The signs are not deceptive: death is near. Not the death of Christianity, but the death of Western, feudal, bourgeois Christendom. A new Christendom will be born tomorrow, or the day after, based on new social groups and new extra-European grafts. We must not stifle it with the cadaver of its predecessor.[7]

It is not a matter of Catholicism appropriating new values and virtues, and making new trophies of them. Religion has rather to be stripped of a whole stifling ideological and sociological context and led back to its essential message, to what theologians call the "kerygma," so that it may take up this new world. Christians must become humble and poor in spirit before approaching this world, with their Gospel freed from a detritus accumulated over the centuries. Montuclard spoke of a double movement of withdrawal and missionary involvement:

How can the Gospel be preached all over the earth if we do not nourish the will to plant it, despite risks and possible persecution, in a world organized on a completely new basis? It is not enough to lament that the Church lost the workers in the nineteenth century. Nor is it enough to praise various missionary initiatives. We must actively desire to remove the obstacles to the Church's mission among the poor, or else have the courage to confess that we prefer Mammon or our comfortable habits to Jesus Christ.

At the same time that we look more boldly—or, at least, more serenely—toward the future, each one of us must rediscover the Church and the Gospel in their true power, which is God's power.

If we want the Christian message to be understood, we must preach the Gospel, not a Christian humanism. If we want people to believe in the Church, we must present it in such a way that it is seen as capable, by its own supernatural means, of bringing a new humanity to life, liberty, fraternity, and the worship of the true God.

Obviously, to succeed in this, we must not depend so much on the opulent riches acquired in the era of Christendom. That day is over. It is wasted effort to support God's action with the methods of Constantine. What we most need to be convinced of is that the Church and the Gospel have no need of any support from political power, nor of any of those means which a false historical ideal, taking the place of an objective analysis of reality, would have us consider indispensable. This whole network of human support around the Church and Gospel is still existent, and has been for a long time in many countries, including France. Also, a great many Catholics still have an idea of Christianity which springs directly from the times of Christendom. For the unbelieving and pagan masses, this is surely an insurmountable barrier. Such nostalgia for the old "Christian order" encourages a mundane wisdom which is always threatening to abandon the absolute character of the faith, the mystery of the Church, the folly of the Cross.

Today's Christian must choose between conserving and converting; between the pure Gospel and a message in which God's wisdom is hidden under the junk of human wisdom; between a Church leaning heavily on the foundations of culture and civilization and a Church whose whole power would come from a living faith, constantly revitalized at the most fundamental sources, in the merciful power of the Lord.

More than ever, evangelization today calls for poverty of

spirit, simplicity of heart, a daily apprenticeship in the Gospels, a theological understanding of Revelation in biblical rather than cultural terms, and fidelity to the action of grace. . . .

We spoke before of choice, but in order for choice to be made, there must be hesitation. Are we still permitted to hesitate?

A whole world is disappearing, and in the process our privileges and securities, all the supports which the Church made for us to facilitate her mission, are becoming things of the past. This world is disappearing, to the advantage of a humanity that has arisen in a new civilization. How could we hesitate in wishing that this disappearance might offer opportunities, still unknown but already certain, for the progress of evangelization? How could we hesitate before choosing to free the Gospel from its fetters, and preparing the presence, in this newborn world, of a Church that would be completely alive to the liberty of the Gospel, centering its teaching, its methods, and its institutions on the sovereign power of grace?

No, we no longer have the choice; we have opted for the Gospel.[8]

The preliminary condition of encounter with this new world is also the first of the evangelical virtues—poverty:

This poverty is not material destitution—although the two are not foreign to each other—but the poverty of spirit that was blessed in the Sermon on the Mount. The poor man of the Gospel is distinguished by a certain detachment in regard to his own ideas and habits, to everything he has previously drawn from his experience and reflection or received from his environment. With pharisaical assurance, the rich man places truth among the goods that he possesses, and since he feels he owns it, he barricades it with his concepts and proofs. But since it is spirit, truth escapes, and the rich man is left with nothing but feeble words, a logic emptied of reality. The man who is poor according to his own spirit of poverty, however, is haunted by the grandeur of truth, and suspects that its dimensions are limitless; since he reveres it with his whole being, he would never want to commit the sacrilege of appropriating it or deluding himself that he has the truth. His whole effort is to be true by letting himself be possessed by it. He sees that truth comes to him from all sides: from a light in his conscience which is like an imprint on him of the face of God; from the Church, who is the mother of truth; and also from another direction, from modern research, all those human initiatives which advance the work of culture and civilization.

God prizes this blessed poverty so highly, and has taken such care to keep men from the pharisaisms of the spirit, that he has not wanted any society, even his Church, ever to be the only channel of truth. The world needs the Church, and the Church needs the world, just as it is true to say, given the plan of Redemption, that man needs an incarnate God, and that, in order to become flesh, God needed man. . . .

The encounter between the Christian world and contemporary values presupposes contacts and sometimes bold commitments. But it especially presupposes poverty of spirit; without it, the result will be only a collision of closed minds or ruinous and unjustifiable concessions.[9]

This, therefore, is the twofold, complementary requirement for renewal: a humble recognition of the values of the modern world, and a movement into this world for the purpose of evangelizing it. This also implies breaking with a moribund Christendom, and returning to the source, the authentic tradition.

Another Dominican, Father Yves Congar, who for some years had been preparing the foundations for this renewal, showed that this "return to the sources" has precedents in the Church:

Most of the reforms the Church has known in the past principally meant returning to the observance of rules which had been fixed in decrees and canons. Yet certain reforms have been made, or at least advocated, in the name of a return to more fundamental sources than these canons, the holiness of which was not questioned. This was the case with the evangelical or apostolic movement that existed all through the twelfth century and which was finally consolidated in the work of St. Francis and St. Dominic. At the beginning of the sixteenth century this was the aim of the reform of John Colet, Lefèvre d'Etaples, Cardinal Ximenès, Erasmus, and others. The present-day reform movement is also of this kind. But what is needed today is not a reforming of abuses, but a revision of structures. And this involves more than merely repealing certain canons, or reinforcing interdicts and censures. (As Mounier said, "An error or a heresy can be refuted, condemned, or extirpated. But you do not refute a drama. . . .") Today's reforms require a return to the very sources, so that deviated forms will not simply be restored, but new forms will be invented. These new forms must be made out of the essential and original spirit, out of the deep tradition of the ever living Church, under the direction of the magisterium.

Sometimes budding reformists are told: Reform yourselves, and everything will be all right; we need men of God first. This is what Father A. M. Weiss said to the reforming trend headed by the Reform-Katholizismus in 1900–1905. At the time the Church was experiencing great internal troubles, while society was enjoying an apparent calm. Today the situation is reversed. No one is questioning the essential structure of the Church; the present reform movement has the benefit of serious preparations, one of the most decisive being the strengthening of the Church's doctrinal tradition in its resistance to modernism. But the present state of affairs and the very nature of the conditions for evangelization imposed by the modern world cause serious doubts about what we may call the structures of the forms of expression of the Church. We do not want to find the solution to this problem outside or against the Church's tradition, but rather in its very depths.[10]

The Testimony of Abbé Depierre

"New forms will be invented. . . ." When these words appeared, the priests of the Mission de France, and the priest-workers (to be mentioned later) were already living in these new forms. One of them was Father Depierre, who worked in the suburbs of Paris. In 1946 he wrote an astonishing article which could be considered a sort of prophetic manifesto for the encounter between the Christian and modern worlds. Their values and virtues no longer had to be reconciled; men already lived as Christians in the most difficult of atheistic worlds, and their experience, as we shall see, tested the whole Church in its practices, words, and states of mind. The Gospel lived again in the midst of a world which it had forgotten; and Christians themselves rediscovered the freshness and truth of the first message. Hope was incarnate.

The Church, like the world which is her body, is experiencing a crisis of growth. She lacks the human contribution which she needs to be alive, "catholic," and which she must love, member by member, trend by trend, giving it her spirit, unity, and purpose. The new world, which is just beginning to explore its new strengths and dimensions, has not yet found its personal conscience, its age of reason. We are coming to the springtime of the world, reinstated in the one, catholic Church.

As a son of this new world and active member of the Church, I have felt in and around me the pulse of life. Perhaps the grace of my priesthood has made me press closer to the powerful heart of the Creator, the eternal and ever present source of Life, so as better to sense its vigorous pulsations. Perhaps the mission of the Church, which has bound my destiny and life to the destiny of the young masses (who yesterday were the marching wing of the Liberation, and today have a similar role in the working movement), has made me more sensitive to the divine life of him "in whom and by whom all has been made and who is the light of every man who comes into this world." Perhaps by letting myself be drawn into the current of the swarming waters of a city in gestation I have better perceived the Spirit hovering over them. At any rate, as a son of a peasant and priest of the Catholic Church, having become a worker among the workers of my quarter, sharing by my destiny and friendship in the uncertainty and peace, the revolt and hope, of my brothers, I seem to perceive in my community the still-sluggish soul of the world remade into the unity of the Church. Believers or unbelievers, young or old, Communists or humanists, we are discovering our unity, sincerely loving each other more and more, sharing food and ideas. We feel free of preconceptions and conformism, strong with the living traditions of the past, and committed together, beyond divisions and easy refusals, to the building of the fraternal city.

We are at the beginning of the renewal of the world, and

we are abusing language if we say that this modern world has been born without the Church. The modern world is still in search of itself, and will remain so until, through the dynamic presence of Christians, the smiling countenance of God has guided its imperfect and scattered efforts. . . . Christians will have to have pure enough hearts to see God where he makes himself known. Until then, men of every persuasion will clash without realizing that, weighed down by innumerable errors, they are all advancing toward the same renewal, and reveal the same absence of divine love. The modern world has not found its unique soul because it has not found the Church.

The evidence of fellow workers who have caught a glimpse of this evangelical vision is unanimous. They wait or they pray. The other day Mauricette and Pierre, two young Communist leaders who were baptized a year ago in the main square of their district, were telling me as they brought back a borrowed Bible: "We have to work together to bring about our Great Evening, in order to rid the world of its inherent sin of injustice, but that will only be the beginning. We Christians will then have to bring love and faith to prepare for the dawn of a New Earth where God will be among us." This expresses a desire implicit in my whole city. But most people, understandably, do not yet know that Catholics are capable of effecting, here and everywhere, the reinstatement of the world into communes, or of making over the Church to the measure of men and the universe.

Among my comrades—whether Christians, Communists, or simply fellow workers—I have found the echo of the often inaccurate prophetic appeals (but isn't this the price to be paid for prophecy?) of the great men of the last century, and I have shared their hopes with all the strength of my actions and with all my priestly faith. Like them, I have responded to Woodrow Wilson's appeal: "I feel that the time has come when men, forgetting purely local ties, should unite in a great undertaking which will join free men together forever." I have also responded to Marx's cry, "Workers of the world, unite!" and to the many appeals of Leo XIII and Pius XI. Christ's prayer, "that they may be one," will slowly be fulfilled if we remember that those who truly transform men are always those in whom the spirit of their environment and their age burns most intensely.

In the first months of my "human" priesthood, I saw my comrades display a real interest in the dream of universal brotherhood. After work we used to go off whistling the refrain of a revolutionary song, to meetings about the social problems of Russia, China, Germany, or America. The carpenter in my apartment house would take me along with his friends to demonstrations for the freedom of Egyptians, Spaniards, Indo-Chinese. Once, a mother of three, an ardent Communist, radiantly showed me the collection taken up in her factory for the hungry children of Holland. When such things happened, I understood that all these people would find themselves too constrained by our homilies, churches, and moral exhortations about individual salvation. In the present time, only St. Paul's faith in cosmic salvation or St. Augustine's in the City of God would be adequate to baptize this need for collectivism and universal Redemption. . . . I also understood that the "catholic" faith was not first of all a personal tie between the soul and God, but a commitment to Jesus Christ, Savior of the World, and a participation in his work of creation and love. I understood that one belonged to the Catholic Church only if one belonged to humanity, for the Body of Christ is made up of the whole of humanity, animated by his life. . . . And I understood that these people would never kneel before a God who would make the world smaller, less alive, less interesting than the one which is open today to their heart and intelligence.

Thus on my knees I reread the first chapters of Genesis: what immense perspectives, what undefined possibilities God opens to these men whom he creates in his image and likeness, and whom he commands to subdue and dominate the earth. Today the means of communication and observation have added antennae to their senses; scientific discoveries have multiplied the strength of their limbs; the great human currents, Asiatic, Slavic, Western, have enlarged their needs for brotherly communion to the limits of the earth. And so the Bible teaches me that they are only responding to God's command. "Extend yourselves," he told his patriarchs, "to the shores of the Oceans, and may your children be as numerous as the sands of the beaches." Have we preserved the strong, human, and eternal meaning of the Word of God? The friends I have made in workshops and bars have made me turn toward the one whom I called, unknowingly, the Almighty. The "communards" with whom I live have restored to my priesthood the hope and vision of a cosmopolitan Pentecostal Jerusalem, of a renewed earth, and a salvation finally refound.

The dimensions of my worker priesthood, of my religious action, of the sacrifice of the Mass, are extended for me to the spiritual life of these men, who have spontaneously united for the completion of the world. They are still unaware that, as sons of God, they are adding "their effort to what is lacking to the passion of Christ" (St. Paul), for the extension of his Kingdom. They do not know this because we Christians of little faith and love have not been on their side. Our ethics, our liturgy, our dogmatics, our very priesthood have no means of entering into their lives. When they do accept them, it is something gratuitous, a superficial veneer. For example, when we force our workers to come to Mass on Sunday morning, we forget that in the winter this is their only morning for sleeping late, and in the summer their only morning for gardening and resting with their families. That is the way they obey the Almighty's command: "Sanctify the seventh day by rest." Last night an old and holy country priest told me, "We are on a higher level than they; we cannot communicate with them; we can neither be true nor sincere." Who, then, is going to tell these men: "You are the sons of our God"?

How did the barbarian world of the Middle Ages become "Christendom"? The rough men of those times, guided by monks and bishops, their brothers and fathers, knew how to clear the land, group the first villages, establish civil codes, and for the first time create a truly mutual and universal peace. They catalogued their material riches, organized the means of life, dominated egoistic passions, made "communes" of their villages, and built cathedrals as their common houses out of the abundance of their hearts and intelligence. . . . Monks, remaining peasants, cleared the land and organized villages. Monasteries were laboratories of progress and theological thought. Theology was— in the intellectual framework of the time—the very consciousness of God and of his living relations with the world. The Middle Ages came into existence only through the Church, and this Church became a Christendom only because it took everything on itself, penetrated and animated everything with the conscience of the time. Freed from its Gallo-Roman shell, it felt the collectivist appeal of the barbarians, and, refining it, guided their material labors and spiritual endeavors in Christian communities. The Church was then the "light of the world," thanks to the involvement of its contemplatives in the life of their contemporaries; and it used constraint against error only as an

*instrument of understanding and love. It directed toward
God the desires of a secular civilization, leading the forward march of the barbarians for the renewal of the West.*

*As a peasant I have felt the stifling weight of contempo-
rary individualism. The application of Roman law to the
notion of property has supported it until there is hardly any
communitarian effort in the villages any more, and less and
less disinterestedness and prayer in work. . . . As a worker I
have seen that even in the poor quarters the law of "I mind
my own business" reigns supreme. It is the fundamental
principle of the organization of work, the family, and living
arrangements, making communitarian exchange impossible. Civil law, urban development, and our basic economic
structures are contaminated at their source because the
spirit of charity has been absent from the human development of our world.*

*Without a Church to guide their faith as well as their
struggle for progress, men are quickly lost. Fortunately, the
suffering of humanity—dying of its lack of soul—has
sharpened its desire for salvation.*

*But men have not found the Church because the latter is
absent from the rhythm of their new life and from the field
of vision of their spirit. They have built themselves entirely
different churches, depending on time, race, and place—
churches where interest has replaced morality, force has
been substituted for love, and demagogy has taken the
place of the Word of God. Why do we reproach these men?
Why condemn hungry children who have not found bread?
Religion has seemed a stranger in their lives and irrelevant
to their salvation. One has to suffer the organized slavery of
the proletariat in order to understand Lenin's despairing
words: "Religion is the opium of the people."**

* This remark is originally ascribed to Bruno Bauer. (Trans.)

Religious peoples such as the Moslems and the Orientals have disdainfully rejected the message of the Whites. This rejection has also taken place in our industrial cities where the mechanized mind seems to have affected the conduct of worship and the very religion of the faithful. I remember a Communist mother saying to her daughters at a religious ceremony: "These people believe in nothing. Remember your uncle who was in Buchenwald and who looks down from above." Would their cause be more religious than our services? Consider this letter written by a Communist father to his daughter, who had told him of her baptism: "Become a Christian if they help you to see and realize better your role as a militant for humanity. But faced with the indifference of the Church, we will find a real mystique which meets our needs and saves the world. Your little sisters will know this and will no longer need baptism to be real Communists." And then there is the comment of André and Jacqueline whose cultured and revolutionary souls, filled with adoration, were shocked by the narrowness and emptiness of Catholic worship. Asking me for baptism at the age of twenty-five, they had for the first time encountered Christians who "believe in God and the salvation of the world. . . ."

Riveted as we Christians are to the idea of individual salvation, to the acquisition of individual virtues (as my friend Alexander always tells me, "What egoists Chrsitians are!"), we have forgotten that faith is an involvement in Christ's redemptive work, in the light of the Revealed God.

Faith is a new birth, a new vision of things and men seen through the eyes of God. It is neither the exaltation of a feeling, the taking of a stand against other men, nor the passive acceptance of a cultural and moral code. This is how St. Paul explains his faith:

To me, though I am the very least of all the saints, this
grace was given, to preach to the Gentiles the unsearchable
riches of Christ, and to make all men see what is the plan of
the mystery hidden for ages in God who created all things; that
through the church the manifold wisdom of God might now be
made known to the principalities and powers in the heavenly
places. This was according to the eternal purpose which he has
realized in Christ Jesus our Lord, in whom we have boldness
and confidence of access through our faith in him . . . that according to the riches of his glory he may grant you to be
strengthened with might through his Spirit in the inner man,
and that Christ may dwell in your hearts through faith; that
you, being rooted and grounded in love, may . . . know the love
of Christ which surpasses knowledge, that you may be filled with
all the fulness of God (Ephesians 3:8–19).

We Christians must understand that faith is not a personal psychological problem but the total involvement of
our being in the Church—that is, in the completion of the
world which has been saved, as we know, by Jesus Christ.

There is need of a morality, not of a moral order. I have
always been struck by the way the masses spontaneously
reject a "moral order" proposed by the Establishment, no
matter how attractive it may seem. The ones who want it
are those who see it as a protection for their privileges. All
the others, the poor in spirit, those who hunger for justice,
detect in it almost instinctively the worst form of the
"world's sin," since any order that would conform to
morality must first preserve truth and justice (which are
two names for God in the Old Testament). A true human
order is realized only when all men are happy and free. A
just order must call for equal rights and brotherly relations
among everyone. We Catholics must stop treating the pro-

letariat, even in our thoughts, as "minors." True education wishes to treat others as they ought to be treated, and so requires a basic trust and true love for all. We know that this active education of men is long in coming. Waiting for it, we must imitate God's four-thousand-year-long patience with his chosen people.

To impose a moral order is to reject a priori men's right and duty to construct their own city, to make their revolution themselves, and to participate as active members in their Redemption. It is only when men are free that morality can be the progressive harmonization of all human freedoms, in a common effort for world unity. God's commands are then seen to support the purpose presumed in the first two commandments: the establishment with God, by all, of the fraternal city.

A world in gestation demands an end to confession-by-formula, based on an egocentric examination of conscience. Otherwise, our reason for living is not as worthy as that of Socialist militants, who are motivated by an ideal of fraternity in social relations and a passion for a human civilization which would gradually make men more conscious of their grandeur.

We are told to safeguard morality in a society which is not free to be moral because it is under external control, forced into a prostitution of hands, work, health, heart, and family. The proletarian world is essentially a city in which the necessities of living hold millions of people captive, whereas the purity and generosity of these modern publicans would quickly place them in the front ranks of free men.

They tell us to safeguard personal freedom, when half of mankind is under a system in which the profit of a few or economic imbalance may annihilate its chance of living humanly. Property rights are held sacred, although the

property of the rich is an anonymous means of oppression,
whereas the parceled-out property of small farmers, divided
every generation, prevents them from learning new techniques and acquiring the possibilities of stability and progress. . . .

We condemn the revolutionary spirit of the masses without realizing that it is the organic and sane human reaction
against a society which destroys spiritual values. The struggle for survival, the underhanded hiring procedures, the
inhuman conditions of work and housing—all these things
prevent millions of men from becoming conscious of their
dignity and their spiritual destiny. The leading supporters
of this system are most often respectable people, prudent
moralists, and contributors to church building drives. No
longer sharing the fate of the poor, Christians support, in
the name of so-called sacred principles, a morality of
egoism and injustice, of weak resignation or morbid despair.

This problem was faced during the Nazi Occupation,
when genuine Christians rose up to defend honor and freedom because they were part of the suffering French community and were themselves victims. Today, confronted
with a socioeconomic system which reduces the proletariat
to slavery, the Catholic conscience unfortunately does not
consider itself part of the suffering community of workers;
humanity, therefore, is organizing itself without Catholicism, and without the hope that all its efforts may con-
verge in a unique salvation.

Pius XI's warning—"The mortal sin of the Church in
the nineteenth century is that it lost the working class"
—ought to be enough to make Catholics humbly understand the necessary shift in their efforts, even if this means
breaking laws. The first Christians and the first popes were
condemned as "enemies of the Roman order." And this
was for having remained faithful to the Revelation of the

Son of God by witnessing, even to the point of martyrdom, to the Creator's love for his redeemed creatures. . . .

Today's Christians should be able to verify that the faith of the proletariat in universal salvation, their unshakable hope, and their fraternal union are not only the driving forces of the worker movement but the greatest moral and spiritual values of our time. And in the future, thank God, these values will be the natural bases of the three theological virtues in a Church which has again become "catholic." If not, the proletariat, suffering because they cannot be men, will again start on a crusade without the Church— and, consequently, without knowing their redeemed destiny as sons of God.

Men today demand the possibility of a free and conscious moral life. This means they must become conscious again of their divine origin and redemption. They need to know that they are saved. Then, without resorting either to the promise of a reward that is more calculated than eternal, or to an egoistic fear of hell, they will discover their personal dignity and unity in the Spirit which makes the world move toward the heart of the Father who created them in his image. They will never accept a morality which, by imposing arbitrary rules, prevents them from creating their world of free and communal men. For them, every morality of this type is an unbearable burden on the shoulders of the people, imposed by pharisees who do not lift a finger to help. As we know, Christ preferred the sinful but humble and brotherly life of the publicans to this type of code, no matter how pure and demanding it might be.

I have never seen a pagan ask for baptism without immediately pledging as completely evangelical a life as possible. The demands of Christianity are not frightening to

men who search sincerely; what such men reject is the
juridical formalism and the hypocrisy of Christians. . . .

A rebirth of Christian conscience will take place when
men rediscover the biblical notion of "the just man, the
righteous man," redeemed by God. Life will have a unity;
there will no longer be separation between its religious,
social, and personal dimensions. Conscious and free choice
will become possible in politics and religion. Everyone will
have a chance to be consistent, as men and as Christians,
finding the source of a personal moral life in a living faith
and in the harmonization of their efforts with those of their
fellow men.

Sin is, above all, the refusal to join the common effort, to
enter the circuit of men's charity. I have noticed that new
converts from the working class always accuse themselves
of personal laxity with regard to the welfare of others and
of the Church. For them, any fault which is not a fault
against their brothers and against the Church is not a "sin."

There will be a re-evaluation of the positive notion of
love, and of love between men and women. According to
God's design, real participation in the common work of
creation begins with the gift of self, in the communion ad
extra realized by man and woman in marriage. The sin of
impurity exists only if it is a sin against love, against the
dignity of others, or against the gift of God—that is, as a
refusal. True chastity and evangelical virginity are only
wider avenues of love for the sake of spiritual action in the
Church. In this way Christians have rediscovered, adored,
and praised the Holy Trinity, which is the communion and
gift of God in himself, source of the Spirit without which
the Father is not Creator, nor the Son the Redeemer.

The sin against the community, against the catholic
Church, is measured properly only against the grandeur of
God and the immensity of his love. The personal sin of the

guilty man becomes insignificant compared with the hindering of Redemption and the holiness of God, who thereby loses one of his points of entry to humanity. Sin is a desanctification of the world and of one's self. It is thus not only a possible condemnation to a hell beyond this life, but also helps to make earth a hell by creating obstacles for Redemption and locating the sinner in the sterile solitude of one damned in this world. . . .

Why, after a meeting at which several genuine Christians had shown that they were deeply committed to revolution, and sustained by a love and faith which were as immense as God and humanity, did eight nonbelievers come to ask me, awkwardly and inaccurately, for baptism, the sacrament of commitment? Why have so many men at war or in my city asked their priest comrades for baptism for their children, or for absolution for themselves? Why have so many fellow workers or technicians, either baptized or Christians without knowing it, asked for the consecrating act which would "confirm" them in their adherence to the Redemption of Christ the Savior? Why are the men of my factory, my bar, my apartment house, gradually approaching our altar, having discovered Christian brothers united and gladdened at the eucharistic meal? Once they have found that an acquaintance or a fellow worker is a Christian priest, why do men come to pour out their intimate lives to him? Why have militant workers whose revolutionary faith I shared wanted to call me "Father, [since] even if you are a priest, you are not like the others; you are more than my father and mother, more than the cell leader, more than the doctor, a man for all seasons"? Why, proud and conscious of the nobility of matter, on which they labor each day, have they so often delegated me to make a handsome offering of it, along with their lives, their tools, and their efforts? Why have men, on the day that, together with their wives, they discovered the eternal grandeur of love, wanted to consecrate it by an act of religion, and to make a solemn declaration to the community that they were married? (Church weddings, however, would be very expensive.)

The answer is that these great human realities, once taken over by Christ and changed into precise means of divine entry into humanity, need to be established on a solid, eternal, and mysterious basis, because they are limitless. There is need of the divine presence in the great decisions of life; need of the Almighty—who may otherwise be ignored—to assure the stability of love and friendship, personal renewal, family meals, and the purpose of one's work.

We need fewer sacraments of the dead, and more sacraments for life—the sacrament of commitment to the Redemption of the world, of adult awareness of Christian responsibility, of love, of the common meal, and, provided it rediscover its humanity, of the priesthood.

The sacraments are ways of access to an eternal vision of the world. They should reinforce contact with God through both an emphasis on faith, and greater religious and liturgical realism. And like all the acts of modern man, they will no longer be conditions of individual salvation, but communitarian acts of commitment to Christ. (For example, public community baptism, Masses, and confession and accusation before others.)

The revealed word of God comes to a close in the Apocalypse with a great processional of unity brought about by the victory of Christ. A Karl Marx was needed to take this hymn and teach it to the modern masses. Faith in a saved humanity, regenerating hope in the new earth, universal and constructive charity—these are the three theological virtues which the workers revealed to me. I am reminded of the breathing of the Spirit in Genesis, of the

prologue of St. John, of the cosmic vision of St. Paul represented in the image of the growing Body of Christ.

This helped me understand the meaning of these struggles for a new era in which slaves will become men; in a
world made over by Christ's Redemption, every tear will be
wiped from our eyes (Apocalypse). We Christians need to
be reborn. Unless we are, this revolution will continue to
reject a Church whose spiritual forces have been exploited
so as to excuse every form of egoism and materialism. In its
very genesis, humanity is revolutionary; redeemed by
Christ, it constantly assaults original sin and "the sin of the
world," whatever it may be. Redemption is a perpetual
combat, the endless effort of humanity against the internal
evil which stifles it.

Why, then, are we so quick to condemn the songs of joy
and deliverance sung by Socialists? Are we really more
open to the "Spirit who renews heaven and earth" than
those who hunger and thirst for justice? Why does our well-
known charity—sometimes accepted, but always resented
by the poor—concern itself only with individual suffering,
not loving men enough to demand, in a world which they
had renewed, honor, a free conscience, and justice for all?
No longer living the life of the poor, have we lost the meaning of the word "savior"? Why have we not loved the dialectic of the world's movement as well as our Communist
companions? Why reproach Marxists for their desire for an
earthly paradise, as if God had not made the earth a paradise first, as if the Savior had not "redeemed the world's
sin"? If we had shared the anguish and hope of the new
men and been human priests, we would have been asked to
enlighten and unite them, not be rejected like strangers and
representatives of a spiritual tyranny. . . .

Our mission as priest-workers has made it clear to us
that a new world is in search of itself. It has not found its

unity, its self-awareness, and its goal, because it is not vivified by the Church, and its great needs correspond exactly to the mission of the Savior, which the Church was founded to continue.

What, then, should be our attitude as Christians and as priests? . . .

First of all, the Church must be present in contemporary struggles and sufferings. This is the humble and "catholic" meaning of the love of Christ, who lived a hidden life among his fellows as a carpenter, so that later he was not recognized by them; and who in his public life was divine enough to be with all of them, giving confidence to publicans and teachers, peasants and soldiers, Jews and pagans, Samaritans and prostitutes. . . .

A true community is slowly taking shape in my apartment house, where all the tenants are workers and unbelievers. Everyone shares our spirit because, doors always open, eating, working, praying, I have shared their life. As priest I have done them the honor of offering Mass in their midst, in my room or in the carpenter's yard. Even the housewives of my quarter, mostly Communists, got together after marketing to ask me to say my Mass with them and their husbands in the square on Saturday afternoon, the workers' day off. After all, the parish church closes just when the workers go home. Why do we priests delay in assuming, as we should, the whole of their life, excepting sin, in imitation of Christ? (St. Paul) In becoming incarnate, God wanted to be called "Emmanuel," "God with us." The function of the Christian is to go and search in the depths of the infinite crowd for the unknown man who believes he is alone, and help him to share again in the divine rhythm of catholicity.

In the village where I was born, as well as in my present district, it is obvious that most Catholics leave it to monks and priests to carry on the work of the Redemption through their suffering, their apostolate, and prayer. When these Catholics say "the Church," they are thinking of priests and work done by the clergy. They merely put up with liturgical prayer and moral instruction. They do not know that they themselves are irreplaceable, responsible, and living members of the Body of Christ. They have forgotten the commitment of the sacrament which consecrated them "soldiers of Christ," just as priests often forget the sacrament of Holy Orders which made them delegates for all men. Irresponsible Christians, they no longer know that beyond its established political appearances, despite the immense crowds it can bring together, the Church of Christ is only what they, its members, are within themselves.

Irresponsible and passive in the Church, do these Catholics no longer feel the life of the city, the exuberance of its hope, the vitality of its youth? They are isolated from those who are materially and spiritually constructing the city of men. It is important that these Christians try to live in a more catholic way. The union achieved by these living members, themselves bound to all their revolutionary comrades who are not yet consciously Christian, could be the Church of the universe.

Involved with all their brothers who are not baptized in Jesus Christ, Christians will take on the life of the world only if they are contemplatives, men overflowing with God. How did this alienation between contemplative and active lives come about? When did farmer-monks disappear? When did theologians and technicians, apostles and leaders of the community separate their prayer from their life? Listen to the anguish of the newly baptized who ask for priests who would be saints: "In my factory, in the midst of frequent contacts with Marxists and militant workers, I have become more aware of my deficiencies, while also understanding better the absence of the true priest: a loving and pacific man, witness of a God in anguish because men need help. . . ." Listen also to the urgent recommendation of Abbé Godin when he founded the "Mission of Paris": "Would that all the missionaries who dedicate their lives to the Christianization of the workers' world were first of all contemplatives." Without this contemplative dimension, the Western world—workers, peasants, intellectuals, scientists—like the Hindus or Moslems, will seek elsewhere for the "good news. . . ."

What has caused this renaissance of humanity? Is it the necessity of helping one another in these wretched times? Has the activity of political cells made a "commune" out of my quarter? The laundress speaks to every passer-by and gives credit to clients. The old Communist across the way, who was yesterday an informer on our activities, now shares the reserves of his little garden with us. The mother whose children are at school will stand in line at the market for her busier companions. The yard of my building is becoming a garage for all the artisans on the street whose workshops are too small. Our meals, which begin with five guests, end up with twelve. . . . There is not a house where the priest cannot come, as companion or visitor, to eat, smoke a cigarette, or ask a favor. He is at home with them, and he knows that, with the grace of God, they will eventually be part of "his" prayer, "his" Mass, "his" Church. Yet no Catholic movement or organization has been started. People vote pretty much as they did before the war. On the fourteenth of July, when an enthusiastic crowd plants the "tree of liberty" on the church square, the parish curé will close his shutters and probably his mind to their songs and frenzy. But these things are not very important, since in a few neighborhoods the "commune," and through it, the "Church," is already alive.

Honor, the feeling for the inalienable dignity of others, the true communitarian conscience, was brought into the world by the Church. . . .

Take Dédé, the leader of an underworld gang; he has given it all up because "It would be stupid to act like that when parents and friends trust us. Nevertheless, I don't believe in either God or the devil, and I really like to give the cops a workout."

What is valued is not reputation and esteem (those primary and essential virtues of the conservative code) but respect for the dignity of others. Adolph, who has found an honor and a conscience that oppose the morality of the "world," summed it up: "I don't hate capitalists, but I have an anticapitalist faith. That's why, when I steal, I explain the reason for my act to my victim, and I never keep a penny for myself. But the families who benefit will never have to know that I stole to help them." More and more, there are those who remain unbelievers, for whom the fault which does not strike at the dignity of their brothers is not a fault. Isn't this a distant, unconscious, yet profound, echo of St. Paul's "Do not conform to this world," or "Do not sadden the Holy Spirit in you"?

For Christians of our community, this spiritual discovery has another aspect. Several have already asked to be publicly excluded from gatherings on a provisional basis, and even from Mass. They have thus excommunicated themselves from the society of the baptized because they feel unworthy or at odds with a moral precept which is too harsh. Refusing the right to call themselves "Christian," they ask only to do penance and pray, until the day when, in front of their brothers, they will find themselves redeemed. These men have taught me what the primitive Church called "public penance."

Baptized and confirmed freely, or else reintegrated at twenty or twenty-five into the life of a religion that they had never before known, the Christians of my neighborhood have become aware of their responsibilities and have heard as new "Be ye perfect. . . ." They want a priesthood in their midst which is involved in their fate, their work, and their prayer. The priest has become one of them again, in preparation for the day when the community will choose the best of its children and humbly propose him for consecration by the bishop. Already we are seeing the man emerge slowly among the workers who, singlehearted because of his total openness and the absoluteness of his commitment, will be the one best able to take on the role of Christ and become the sign of union among men, the one chosen to pray and offer sacrifice, the father of the people. In my quarter, it used to be the Communist mayor or the Socialist inspector of hygiene who took on this "episcopal" role. But now their city requires a man who is more free, and, above all, more religious. Pierre himself asked if the Cardinal would give him priestly consecration for the factory where, in fact, he is the priest. There would also be Riton, for his quarter; Loulou, for the political movements which he unites; Jean for his group of bars. I promised them that in the future the Church would choose them without taking them out of the milieu in which God had made them priests, and would consecrate them to represent her there. Already they show in their conduct and example what the passion for the world, transformed by the love of Jesus Christ, can do in man. They have chosen the holy and priestly vocation of mixing with the workers of the world, for the love of Christ, to complete his work. Already we see sons of the modern world arising—technicians, workers, doctors, militant Socialists—who claim the priesthood for their community, knowing that their human efforts and their natural conquests nourish souls and make the body of Jesus Christ grow to plenitude.

The liturgy is the sublime expression of a faith which no longer fears science, technology, or progress. It is an unlimited trust in man at the service of his brothers, and in humanity regenerated by its Savior. The liturgy is the most beautiful way of going beyond human effort, and a sign of completion of the world. From natural forces to the men who make use of them, from these men to the believers gathered from among them, from the Christian community to the priest, the life of the modern world ascends to its Creator through Christ who divinizes it.

We have finally found "better songs to sing" to the world, and disciples of the Savior who look more as if they had been redeemed.[11]

II

A Mission Country

Facing Facts

The re-examination occasioned by the Occupation of France was not simply a reflection on values. Priests began to discover a reality that habit and traditional vocabulary had kept hidden. France, "eldest daughter of the Church," was a country two-thirds dechristianized. The JOC (Young Christian Workers) chaplains had already had some idea of this cruel truth. Now hundreds of priests were forced to respond to crisis situations and work in environments with which they were unfamiliar: in Germany, with imprisoned soldiers, then with deported workers; in the Maquis, with young people who were mostly atheists, including many Communists. A thirty-six-year-old JOC chaplain, Abbé Godin, made a striking formulation of this discovery by calling the book he wrote with Abbé Yvan Daniel *France*, *pays de mission?* Its publication in 1943 unleashed a real storm. The book presented the facts of the dechristianization of industrialized areas, particularly around Paris:

In the actual state of things conversion presents for the ordinary worker difficulties comparable with those experienced by a pagan in a foreign mission. He has not only to leave the evil things in his life—he has to leave his life as a whole: his friends, his relatives, his customs, his Sunday outings; he must change his manner of life. He has been living in a proletarian world; he must leave his world.

To ask this of him is to ask for heroism—to a degree that we cannot imagine. Small wonder that many hesitate, that some recoil.

They are leaving what they know, leaving what has made them; and, as they look at it, our parochial world seems to them timorous and shrunken, terribly *bien pensant*, terribly old-maidish. It seems to them (I have heard this so often, false though it is, that I hope I may be excused for setting it down here), it seems that to love Christ they must accept a lowering, a lessening of their personalities. They are men, tough men, workers. They hate the "inferiority complex" of the "pious" Christian.

Nor is this all. What makes the difficulty greater is that what Christ wants is not only individuals—he wants numbers. And here we face not merely a difficulty, but an actual impossibility. For the average man in any community does not live alone; he will never abandon his milieu unless others go with him. Indeed he will never abandon it at all; he is not the man to run the risk of losing his place in his own society with all its consequences. Even with the young this is true, although in differing degrees. For adults, for family groups, it is a sociological rule—with very occa-

sional exceptions, but with the same sort of over-all verifi-
cation as a law of physics or biology.

But here the reader may well be asking: Why postulate
as a necessity that the converted proletarian must abandon
his milieu?

The answer is that the parish and the proletarian worlds
are not merely separated, they are also utterly different.
Parochial Christianity, reconstituted in France during the
birth of the middle classes, possesses its own culture:
Catholic, of course, but soaked through with a bourgeois
mentality, colored by bourgeois qualities and by bourgeois
defects. A great preoccupation with what is "respectable,"
a concern with refinement in appearance and in speech, a
sense of order, good administration, well-run accounts, a
certain good taste. All these smaller virtues, useful in finding a place in life and starting a family, are apt to look pale
and ungenerous when transferred into the Christian and
apostolic field.

And in practice these lesser virtues often enough issue in
an individualism which shirks community effort—which,
for instance, rejects liturgical prayer because it calls for the
participation of all, which feels repugnance against becoming a militant in a movement organized for Christian conquest.

Then, too, for the proletarian the whole exterior side of
worship presents its difficulties—the class distinctions in
marriage ceremonies and funeral processions, hired altar
boys, payment for chairs, the opening and shutting of
churches, the material externals; the very services that
should draw him to the church and keep him in it have
ceased for him to be common prayer; he does not understand them at all.

I remember a solemn All Saints' Day in a suburban
parish. There were Vespers of the feast, Vespers of the
dead, recitation of the Rosary, Benediction of the Blessed

Sacrament. It lasted for two hours, and not one word was in French except the Rosary. A professional choir sang to an "audience" of some three hundred—and that number was considered remarkable as being much higher than usual. The clergy were in their stalls, the altar blazed with electric light. This parish had in its care more than fifty-five thousand souls. In the streets an animated crowd milled back and forth full of vitality, with long queues outside every cinema. Three hundred in the church; the rest outside. The contrast moved me to tears.

Try then to imagine our proletarian coming into a parochial milieu. Too often we treat him rather as a missionary would who chose to begin by teaching a pagan French, putting him into European dress, teaching him our manners and customs, when he should be teaching him the Gospel.

Of course it is easier to teach Christ's religion in such a context. But the question must be asked: Why first convert to a culture and make acceptance of that culture a condition of acceptance of the faith? We are astonished when our pagans hesitate or refuse to come to church. But are we facing the problem in the right way? Should not they create and then live in a Christian community, a Church? Some of our mistakes may arise from our forgetting the true sense of belonging locally to the Church.

In any case let us face the fact courageously: in the mid-twentieth century the faith is not preached in one whole world; millions of Frenchmen have not the Gospel preached to them.[1]

Today it is hard to imagine the shock caused by this revelation. After the Godin-Daniel book was published, many parish inquiries and studies of religious sociology verified this alleged disproportion: Although nearly 85 per cent of Frenchmen were baptized, two-thirds of them

quickly abandoned religious practice and lived as pagans.
Only occasionally did they take part in some solemn feast
(midnight Mass, marriages, funerals). A survey made by
the French Institute of Public Opinion in 1958 established
that young people were divided into three groups: 33 per
cent practicing Catholics, 14 per cent atheists, and 53 per
cent nonpracticing Catholics and others. In addition, the
proportion of practicing Catholics diminished with age,
and was especially low in working-class parishes. At
Montreuil in 1939, only about two thousand people out of
a population of seventy thousand went to Mass on Sunday.

The usual methods of the apostolate were obviously useless in such a situation. The Church had to recognize that
she had again become a minority, like the early Church,
isolated in a hostile—or, worse still, indifferent—milieu. If
France, like Africa, was "mission country," missionaries
should be sent to it. Godin meant to summon them, but
died in an accident in January 1944; and his closest assist-
ant was killed shortly afterward with the Maquis in Savoy.
However, the seed that had already been scattered bore
fruit immediately. Dozens of priests were freed from their
ministry to be assigned to the evangelization of the masses;
the "French Mission" (*Mission de France*) was founded in
1941, with decisive support from Cardinal Suhard of Paris.
The following is an excerpt from his spiritual notebook:

*I am recording a fact: our people as a whole no longer
think in a Christian way. There is a gulf between them and
the Christian community which makes it necessary for us to
leave our environment and go to them. This is the real
problem.*

*Up to now our efforts have been nearly fruitless. It is
well known that our ordinary Catholic Action is impotent.
It is an organization of Catholic neighborhoods, or at least*

of believing ones, not the "Catholic Action of pagan environments."

I understand better now which works of the apostolate are necessary. Despite the zeal of priests, Paris is not sufficiently evangelized, due to lack of effective attention to the non-Christians who constitute the majority of the city's population.

That is the ideal toward which I must orient myself and the souls of priests, the faithful, and, above all, the militants.

A conversion must be effected, a world must be lifted up, and only God can do this, by a direct action on souls.

Am I fit to obtain it by prayers, my sacrifices, my personal action?

For that, one would have to be a saint.

The Church will grow only if she sinks her roots right into pagan soil.

We have to go out to souls in order to save them, but we must also become fearlessly involved, when necessary, in the temporal and social spheres, because the divine will and the law of the Gospel are there too. That is the road whereby many souls can be reached and saved.

We cannot win souls by excommunicating them or by annexing them through indiscreet constraints, even in the name of truth.[2]

Many Christians agreed with this rejection of spiritual pride and apologetics by conquest. One example is found in a letter from the young Jesuit, Henri Perrin, who, after returning from forced labor in Germany, was preparing to rejoin the mission of a working-class district:

The proletarian world, the nonbelieving world, has become as foreign and inaccessible to us as a distant mission land; and, reciprocally, our religion is unintelligible to

*people who chance to enter into contact with our institu-
tions. . . . In a word, we need to strip ourselves of a whole
spirit of clericalism—a clericalism in opposition to the
Gospels.*

*The feeling of being at a dead end, the need for purifica-
tion . . . can be found in numbers of priests, both young
and old. . . . I call to mind a young parish priest in Paris,
poor and loved by his parishioners who are mostly workers
and small tradesmen, who said to me three months ago:
"In the last six years I've done everything for my parish: I
live poorly, my presbytery is open to all, and I know my
people . . . and yet the practice of religion is still falling off.
Why?" Because the forms of Christian life, taken as a
whole, have become empty of meaning for our contemporaries, because the Gospels are no longer "good tidings,"
because the sacraments no longer signify anything, because
we have cut ourselves off from life.*

*That is why the presence of priests really living among
the masses seems to me a necessary condition of reform
and progress. . . . For, without knowing it, we seem at the
moment like people struggling to keep their privileges. We
turn these privileges into rights of Christ, of the Church,
and of truth, but in fact they are mere accidents, although
ones it would be awkward to change. It is because we so
often live in contact with a world where there is no suffering from capitalist injustice that it is vital for us to dive
headlong into the life of the masses. . . .*[3]

A Missionary Church

Cardinal Suhard himself drew a sketch of the new type
of priest that was needed, who would place himself firmly
within the life of his community:

To be a priest suited to the twentieth century is not a matter of slavishly copying methods suited to former times nor of inventing new forms for the sake of novelty, but it means to translate the message of Christianity into present-day terms. Briefly, a priest must adapt himself. It would be a grave mistake, one which is occasionally made, to suppose that this adaptation consists in servile imitation of contemporary customs. It is not because a priest uses the latest technical inventions or because he keeps up to date in his reading that he will ipso facto get his people to listen to him. It is true that today more than ever before he is bound to be in the forefront of thought and culture. But if this knowledge does not proceed from a more profound understanding so that he can sympathize from within with the hardship and the hopes of his brethren, they will not acknowledge him as one of them.

You are now on guard against a too-literal conception of adaptation. Beware then of falling into the opposite and much more serious error which consists in holding that a priest, because he is all things to all men, must never particularize himself, that is, that he must remain aloof from committing himself to human life. That would be the negation of Saint Paul's own principle, "With the Jews I lived like a Jew, to win the Jews; with those who keep the law, as one who keeps the law, to win those who kept the law."

These frequently quoted words define the double task incumbent upon the apostle in general and on the priest in particular; he must renounce some things and take on others. It means renunciation of those things which are peculiar to himself—his education, tastes, culture, and even his native language. But also it means to borrow from those he wishes to evangelize. The essential things are to be given to them, the Gospel and the supernatural life. In turn he

must take on certain of their characteristics, ways of understanding and of feeling previously unfamiliar. . . .

It is a fact that that wall is still standing. Yes, it is a long,
thick rampart dividing into two closed camps the Church
and temporal society. The first duty of the priesthood in
our day is to recognize this fact and to look the world in the
face. It is a formidable sight!

The development of the Church probably for a long time
to come depends on this stopping for a moment, this pause
for silence and prayer. After fifty years of the priesthood,
as on the very morning of his ordination, today's priest asks
himself: In the face of that horizon blurred by the smoke
of factories, in the face of universities and laboratories
which produce as many problems as discoveries, what
should he do? . . . Those workers that he encounters
around the factory gate, how can he become like them,
how can he become their brother?

Hundreds of priests have asked themselves that question.
And many have already answered it. Salvation lies neither
in methods nor techniques. Now is not a time for harvest-
ing but for sowing and, in order to do that, therefore for
understanding. . . .

In too many so-called Christian countries, France in particular, the Church, despite having many churches and
priests, is no longer present to the majority of men. It is no
longer possible for men to choose whether they will be for
or against Christ. An enormous accumulation of prejudice
has utterly distorted the face of the Church in their eyes.
The priesthood is even less accessible to them. So it is fit-
ting for priests to become witnesses again, not so much to
convince people as to serve as a sign to them. It has been
truly said, that to be a witness does not consist in engaging
in propaganda, nor even in stirring people up, but in being
a living mystery. It means to live in such a way that one's

life would not make sense if God did not exist. To be a witness is much less a matter of external changes in one's way of living than of firm determination to establish a real community of destiny with the disinherited masses. The life of these priests is neither an escape nor a means of studying customs, nor even an attempt at conquest; it is a vocation of Redemption. Work is not for them a pretext or an opportunity to propagandize; it is the priest's "naturalization papers" among people to whom he no longer is anything but an alien. . . .[4]

Going still further, Cardinal Suhard declared that it was no use sending off a token vanguard into dechristianized areas: the whole Church had to become missionary.

There are not two clergies, the priest-workmen and the others. The priests who have taken on the full life of the workers should not be thought of as foreshadowing the priestly ministry of the future. But "neither are they free lancers; they are, rather, the vanguard of a clergy which, in its entirety, is moving forward. . . . The Catholic Action laity, priest-workers who are not attached to parishes, and the new missionary parishes, all three of these, then, seem to be necessary. It is all part of the same effort of the Church to put herself on a missionary basis."[5]

Three hundred priests of the *Mission de France* had already been divided into teams and were working in the most dechristianized areas; others were left to work in the poorest countries in North Africa and Latin America.

A brochure edited by the Mission summarized its aims perfectly:

Our mission is to the secular world.

Work and love, science and technique, culture, art, and progress allow man to expand. The world is being transformed and is growing. . . .

In order to be present to the world, we must try to be one with men, to be incarnated in their lives; to be workers with the workers, peasants with the peasants; to share their joys, struggles, troubles, and prayers; to unite contemplation and action by vivifying both; to rediscover the sacred meaning of all things, and make the whole of human life the road which leads to the Father. "Everything is yours, but you are Christ's, and Christ belongs to God."

Our task is evangelical.

We will minister to the poor enslaved by misery; to the rich who are prisoners of their satisfaction; to the hopelessly afflicted and to those who have no cares; to a world torn by hate, dominated by money, and deprived of joy.

To make the Gospel heard, we must bear witness to a virile and brotherly charity, to a voluntary and joyous poverty, to a filial abandonment in the hands of the Father. We must learn the "little way" of Thérèse de Lisieux.

". . . The company of those who believed were of one heart and soul, and . . . they had everything in common."

What we do, we must do as a community.

To overcome the loneliness of the rectory, avoid the dispersal of apostolic efforts and the splintering effect of separate parish projects with common aims.

We must live our priesthood in common. In obedience to the bishop, in liaison with the diocesan clergy, the missionary team takes as its "area" a whole natural sector of human life. Only if we pray together, think together, act together, can we build up a living cell of the Mystical Body.

"For where two or three are gathered in my name, there am I in the midst of them."

Our work is missionary.

We undertake it on behalf of the faithful of all our parishes, but especially for the others—for those deprived of God and unaware of their destiny who are caught up in the mystiques of the day; for the immense crowds of our working masses, as well as for a peasant world bound to the soil.

We wish to announce Christ, to bring his truth into the life of all men. We must be his messengers to family and professional communities, at the crossroads of social relationships, in the centers of influence of the civilization that is now being created. We are to be church builders for a new age, helping Christendom rise up out of a pagan world.

"So there shall be one flock, one shepherd."

Vast sections of the countryside were as dechristianized as the cities. For them there was founded, during the war, a special congregation, the Missionary Brothers of the Fields:

The Congregation was founded in 1943 in a village of Seine-et-Marne, through the initiative of Father Espagneul, a Dominican who specialized in parish missions. By 1962 there were one hundred thirty members, with an average age of thirty-three, and three-fourths with a rural background; nearly half will not be priests, but remain "auxiliary Brothers." They come from fifty dioceses, and are working in about ten, chosen from among the most dechristianized and with the greatest shortage of priests.

In the priory, I met Brother Alfred, who worked on the problem of water supply. "Why does the Congregation get involved in work like that?" I asked. "It's not farming; it's *not something peculiar to this area. It would hardly seem much help in your apostolate.*"

"*We mustn't confuse 'rural' and 'agricultural.' Rural life is quite varied. Our job is to be present in every milieu. We urge each Auxiliary Brother to have a specialty. Many are agricultural workers, but some are carpenters, masons, painters, tilers, and so forth.*

"*Anything having to do with water is an important business to the villages. Of course, the headquarters for the operation is far from here, but part of the day labor is recruited right in the village square. Brother Alfred isn't the only one in his situation. Besides, the workers are always being displaced. Everyone tells them that they don't deserve help because they are 'outsiders.' While the job is being done, they live in our villages. They live in the countryside, often among the local people. They frequent the café, some also spend time with prostitutes. It would be wrong for us not to be concerned with them.*"

"*But wouldn't Brother Alfred be more useful in an apostolic activity?*"

"*What do you mean by that? To be in a human situation, to listen, to answer questions, to try to understand the problems which each one has so as to be more capable of helping him discover Christ. . . . Isn't this the apostolate?*"

"*But there are so few workers in such an enterprise. It's a work without scope.*"

"*Brother Alfred has many contacts—and there is the value of the living witness. You know how tenacious the prejudice against priests is in some places. He is considered someone who lives off others, and is socially useless, if not incompetent. Our Brothers bear witness by doing their work conscientiously, and by their professional competence. People know that they work for a living.*"

During our conversation a truck loaded with bricks arrived in front of the priory. When the village mason went up to receive the merchandise, the driver asked for help in unloading.

"We'll get the Brothers," the mason said, as if it were the most natural thing in the world.

"Brothers?" the driver repeated.

Two of them got there immediately and began working.

The Prior invited me to eat with him. A Brother came in late, excused himself, but did not seem embarrassed.

"That is Brother Bertrand; he's come back from a religious instruction class for children in the main town around here, about nine miles away."

"Is the Brother a priest?"

"No, he's an Auxiliary. Most of them are manual laborers. However, they all get a thorough formation to help them maintain the equilibrium of their religious life. Of course you're surprised. Several of the priests nearby were quite openly upset at seeing an Auxiliary Brother take charge of a religious instruction class in a public school. But now that they have seen them in action they are reassured."

"Why don't these brothers become priests?"

"Because it isn't their vocation. There have always been religious non-priests in the Church. We must get rid of this prejudice that they are second-class religious. But let's go and wash up; they're setting the table."[6]

The Priest-Worker Experiment

The best known of the missionary initiatives has been the priest-workers. Their first inspiration was very close to that of the *Mission de France*, but they soon acquired their own originality and autonomy. They considered having a job an essential part of their priesthood. They wanted to break completely with the bourgeois way of life, and with the priestly routine associated with it. They got themselves hired, most often without revealing that they were priests, in factories and workyards, in the worst of working conditions, in the most impoverished quarters. Soon teams of priest-workers were set up in metallurgy, in the building trades, and on the docks. They have been much written about, but we have few documents on their actual life, since they had neither time nor taste for writing, and wore themselves out trying to live up to all their responsibilities, sometimes including important roles in the unions. This makes all the more valuable the collection of letters of Father Perrin, to which we have already referred, which provides considerable illumination on his day-to-day experience. Here is a letter to his friends in which he discusses a recent strike and tells of the funeral of a fellow worker who died in an accident:

Notre-Dame-de-Briançon,
March 15, 1952

Dear Everyone. Here's another collective letter, which is a way of avoiding repeating the same things over and over again to individuals.

We are now fully out of the strike, and the results regarding my pay are gratifying. I earned 6,000 francs in the last three days; that is to say, for 30 hours' work. But above all, what we have gained is that the management has really got going, that the worksite is running better than ever before, that there are constant adjustments in the organization of the work, and that the "township" is growing under our eyes. Better still, the bosses, far from trying to make reprisals, treat the strike leaders with obvious respect. They consult us and listen to us. In a word, the situation is good.

A new fatal accident that occurred four days after our return to work (one of us was crushed by a tractor in the tunnel) served to reinforce the attitude of the workers and the situation I have just described.

As far as I am concerned, all is well, and Christ seems to be taking a guiding hand in events. From our workmates I get an esteem and trust often amounting to friendship, which overwhelms me and makes me ashamed. The smile and the handshake of our workmates, whether those of the union, or the Spaniards or North Africans, is my best reward and consolation. It would be impossible for me to want to get away soon. The management, too, has started playing the same game. On a number of occasions the manager has come to have talks with me, has told me of his plans, and has asked me what the workers think of them.

The funeral of our workmate also marked a new stage for me. Inevitably, I had to officiate at it myself. All the workers were present, when I appeared all dressed up and ornamented, before a great number of workmates who were not yet aware that I was a priest. Half of them came into church; the other half stayed outside. When we emerged, some of them came up to me and said that in the view of all, or nearly all, the ceremony had increased the trust they felt in me. As in addition to this I've had an opportunity of spending a long evening with the Bishop of Moutiers, I am now in an exceptionally good situation. . . .

I am very tired, but slowly getting better (I'm taking a tonic), and work takes up a lot of time. But this is nothing compared with the expressions of friendship that my workmates are showing me and the possibility of work ahead of us in really good conditions.

I hope you will thank Our Lord, as I do. I shall be praying with you for you all and for all those who are dear to us. . . .

P.S. Here's the latest. On his way back from work the union secretary told me that the undermanager, who is always shouting at others, even by his own admission, told the workers' representatives not to be afraid to shout at the foremen who are not doing their work properly![7]

Another of Perrin's letters shows what the difficulties were for a priest who, without seeking it, took on union responsibility:

Notre-Dame-de-Briançon,
April 1, 1953

My very dear Sister. Thank you for your letter of February 15. I can't blame you for writing so little, because my silence has been just as great as yours, but I want you to get a letter for Easter. . . .

Now for news, as you ask. Our life on the worksite goes on without any great changes, but a thousand-odd incidents to fill it. With evening Mass and our fairly regular priest-worker meetings, the hundreds of problems that arise every day with my workmates bring me into the presence of God. Opportunities are not lacking. As to your question about whether we've managed to get the recreation center going, alas we have hardly any time to think of it. We can hardly ever find a free moment from our work problems (constant disputes about wages, about respect for our liberties, about impending unemployment), and when we do, we are caught up in personal problems, such as the jobless North Africans, family difficulties, and so forth. In the last four months there have been 900 of us at Notre-Dame-de-Briançon, and in all, nearly 2,000 working on the Isère-Arc project. The whole worksite life revolves around and is expressed by the union life; so the people I see are mostly responsible union people. In practice, I am the most re-

sponsible worker on the site, and nearly everyone shows complete trust in me. This is the most impressive, and at the same time the heaviest, side of our life as priest-workers. Many of the men show unlimited affection, which with some of them turns into deep friendship, in which we find all that is best in ourselves.

To give you an example of the sort of problems we are up against: As a result of the 1952 strike, we obtained, among other things, an agreement for a bonus of 60 million francs, of which half had to be paid when the tunnel was through, if this occurred before July, 1953. We got through last week, three months ahead of schedule, so 30 million was distributed within 36 hours at the canteen door. Now you must realize that on pay night some of the boys here are always drunk. I therefore put out a special appeal for dignity, which the workmates applauded. And I was really amazed to see that, in a worksite literally deluged with one-thousand-franc notes, there was not a single drunk in the canteen for two successive nights. On Saturday we held an enormous banquet (1,600 places), and I can't tell you how moved I was to be the only priest and at the same time the man who represented the 1,200 workers present. After the banquet there were a lot of silly fights among the men. I and a few others stood by to separate them, calm them down, and bathe bleeding faces. Then, with the help of another workmate, I had to look after a young North African who was having a nervous breakdown. And so on. Those particular days were exceptional, but there's always something. How in the world could I want to leave these men for the kids of the parish club?[8]

Soon the activity of the priest-workers took a turn which brought their proposed projects, and even their basis for

existence, under scrutiny. The modern world is not a place
where the Gospel must be preached to a backward civilization. Neither atheists nor the workers are easily reached. It
is foolish to think that today's unbelievers are simply waiting for the Word to be preached and their emptiness to be
filled. We are talking about a world which is already "full,"
which has its own norms and mentality, and when it comes
to the workers, its own organization and hope. The early
experience of new missionaries showed them that to be
"Jewish with the Jews, weak with the weak" was to become
deeply attached to this world that had separated completely
from the Church. Was it then necessary to cut ties with
Christianity and naturalize oneself as a worker in order to
be heard by the workers? And how far should this go? Jean
Lacroix, a philosopher of the *Esprit* group, expressed this
crucial problem clearly:

> It is inexact to say, as even we usually do, that the pro-
> letarian masses are dechristianized. Actually the workers'
> universe was born and developed in the nineteenth century
> like a foreign body, without relation to the Church—out-
> side it, not understanding its behavior or mentality or lan-
> guage.This is a fact of tremendous significance and we have
> not yet considered all its consequences. First, it is impor-
> tant that these two universes at least penetrate each other
> and understand each other. At present the priest-workers
> are not capable of converting the workers. They can only
> live among them and in them, as witnesses.[9]

The point of departure was thus reconsidered. This
modern world is defined less by what it lacks, its paganiza-
tion and dechristianization, than by its own certitudes and
values. It is less a question of converting it than of being
converted to it:

The workers' world is not a pagan world. One cannot employ the same methods of evangelization as those used, wrongly or rightly, among the Zulus and Kaffirs. In fact, the worker movement is eliminating two pagan phenomena from the consciousness of its activists which still exist among the sub-proletariat. These are natural religiosity, based on fear of the unknown; and a feeling of impotence, which made the poor assume that any improvement in their lot had to come from their superiors. . . .

In addition, the common struggle and the results already attained by the movement have given militant workers an inner strength and confidence of victory. Everyone who has been close to today's workers has had the extraordinary sense that through the labor movement humanity is finding a new youth, and that it will not find God on the same paths that were followed in earlier times.[10]

The subject of the priest-workers was more and more debated as they settled into urban living conditions and took on responsibilities within the structure of the working class—in unions, mutual-aid associations, and sometimes even political groups. Jean Lacroix emphasized the originality and significance of this experiment for the whole Church:

In itself the idea of priest-workers is debatable. A priest is at everyone's service, and there can be dangers whether he is a teacher, lawyer, doctor, engineer, worker, or peasant. In any case, the priesthood must transcend every employment. The idea of a proletarian vocation is meaningless—it is not on the same plane as the vocation of a priest. Under present conditions, however, the existence of priest-workers is necessary for the catholicity of the Church. Without them, its universality would be in danger. Those

who reproach priest-workers with identifying the Church
with a particular group forget that, despite their poverty,
most priests are either bourgeois or peasant in origin, and
as such are cut off from the entire proletariat. As long as
these conditions remain unchanged, some sort of exceptional vocation will have to make the universality of the
Church visible and sensible. Even if the priest-worker experiment only continues for a short time, they are not an
"accident," but express the very essence of Catholicism.
Religion, which is above all the kingdom of the concrete,
cannot be content with a kind of intellectual universalism.
The idea of mission requires a deep and preliminary rooting in the milieu that is to be evangelized, a community of
life with the people, a marriage to a specific human situation. . . .

The priest-worker must build on a real situation if he is
eventually to transcend it. His position is justified, first of
all, from a pastoral point of view, from which it is most
conveniently examined. Some people would gladly see the
priest-workers as delegates to the proletariat, entrusted
with the task of establishing some sort of bridge between
the middle class and the poor, and preparing the way for
eventual encounters. Apparently concerned with the universality of the priesthood, these people would actually give
priest-workers the more self-interested goal of easing the
class struggle by their mere presence. This is to be completely mistaken about the profound nature of the priest-
worker: he is a worker, and not "among the workers." He
must also accept the workers' condition in its harshest
aspect, its absolute insecurity. His entry into the worker
world is total or it is nonexistent; to penetrate this world of
suffering as an informer or counsellor would be contempti-
ble. Because of the same understanding of the need for
incarnation, priest-workers are led to accept those com-

mitments which are part of the normal life of workers. Not to assume them would be an explicit refusal to take part in their world as it really is. These commitments to the unions are not specifically political, and it would be natural to forbid a priest-worker to belong to a party. It would be arbitrary, however (although acceptable in some circumstances), to prevent him from helping run the union (his superior education and spirituality may be quite useful to his comrades), and absolutely unacceptable to forbid him all participation in union life. It is true that there is risk of being submerged in this duty of incarnation, and proper steps may be taken to prevent this. But it is never a good method to suppress life, just because there is risk of being submerged in it.[11]

To remain completely faithful to the Church while living the life of a worker was a hard task which events complicated still further. The priest-worker experiment developed in France after the unity of the Resistance had been destroyed. The Communist party, which was supported by most workers, was fighting against governments in which the Christian Democrats were major participants. The cold war further hardened positions, until there seemed to be an unbridgeable gap between the majority of French Catholics, who had retreated to prudent and defensive positions, and a small avant-garde. In addition, Vatican support of the experiment seemed to be gradually diminishing. A number of incidents found the priest-workers opposed to the hierarchy, employers, and the police. We cannot present a full history of these events, nor do we wish to judge the participants; our concern is merely to present the ideas which were expressed at the time, and may still provide useful reflection today. These texts will not be understood, however, if the bitterness of the social and political conflict of those days is forgotten. What stands out is the shock felt by these priests, of whom the majority did not come from working-class families, when they discovered among the workers, and especially in the then very powerful Communist party, militants whose poverty and spirit of sacrifice seemed like the early Christians'. Some of them concluded that the future of humanity was linked up with the triumph of these men. What was the good of preaching the Gospel in a corrupt capitalist society which was condemned to death? Was it not more worthwhile to wait for the Communist revolution to create the structures of a just city which the Church could then baptize? This feeling, along with the intellectual appeal of Marxism, helped produce Father Montuclard's theory that it was "the time of St. John the Baptist," the time of silence and preparation; the best way for Christians to hasten the kingdom of God was to work for the coming of the classless society:

We believe that God offers salvation to all men. Therefore, we are sure that the workers' world will not turn away forever from religion. But we recognize that it is becoming more and more atheistic, as there is a decline in natural religiosity, even among those who practice religion. It seems almost certain, moreover, that when faith flourishes again in a revitalized and adult world it will build on different human realities than those in which it has most often been rooted for two thousand years. Until now, faith has usually been connected with the impotence and misery of man. It will appear again only after men—and especially the workers—slowly take possession of their entire humanity. In practice, Christianity preached a salvation which had two aspects: a spiritual liberation and a relative human deliverance. The Church which announced the Kingdom of God was also busy opening hospitals, humanizing wars, creating corporations and unions. From now on men will look to science, mass action, technology, and social organization to realize, on a greater scale, this human deliverance which in the past the Church offered in addition to its spiritual task. Christian salvation will only be able to be presented as man's highest liberty, enlightened and nourished by God. Until now the Church could accept being situated in the infrahuman, but henceforth men will attain this of themselves and will be interested in the Church only after they have conquered the human sphere. . . .

Is socialism the enemy of Christianity? Surely, under present circumstances, there are many facts which give good reason for thinking so. But the Roman Empire also persecuted the Church and refused to believe; it nevertheless created the very conditions which made possible the extension of the Gospel. Will Socialism produce a better human order for the benefit of all men, and through this order create the conditions of a new development of the Church? No one can answer this question today, but can we refuse to think about it? Who would dare deny that the rule enunciated in Pius XII's last encyclical on the Missions also applies to the world of labor? "From its beginning the Church has always followed the wise norm according to which it does not destroy what is good, honest and beautiful among the people who embrace her. . . ." (Evangeli praecones)

What is important to remember is that if we are to safeguard the possibility of a future preaching of the Gospel we must not seek any immediate apostolic result which could confirm in the minds of the militant workers the common objection that religion can survive only among those who are alienated. . . .

If we cannot quite imagine how faith in Christ and the

Church will appear when it rises out of a newly freed proletariat, we at least know clearly its two demands—appropriately contradictory. On the one hand, faith must be separated from all the social-political assumptions to which it has been annexed in the past. At the same time, the believer should be impelled to an effective sharing in the liberation which the proletariat is now patiently leading. It is necessary to be committed and not committed, not successively, but at the same time. Faith is to be set free, but the believer is to be committed. . . .

The human grandeur of Communism shows us that we need to relearn the proper grandeur of Christianity. The historical mission of Communism shows us that we must rediscover the real raison d'être of faith. Otherwise we will never again feel the indispensable pride of being Christians. After we recognize what Communism brings to humanity, we need to be told clearly what Christ will bring to men who will owe their first liberation to Communism![12]

While one could fairly accurately identify the working-class movement with the Communist party in many French industrial regions, this situation did not necessarily prevail elsewhere. The priest-worker movement was consequently in danger of being limited to a particular time and place. By assuming that Communism was the exclusive instrument of history, the Jeunesse de l'Eglise group was led to make concessions to dialectical materialism which were hardly compatible with Christian theology. . . . On February 3, 1952, the Vigilance Committee of the Archbishop of Paris published a warning against Les evénements et la foi, and on October 20, 1953, the Assembly of Cardinals and Archbishops condemned Jeunesse de l'Eglise, which then ceased its activities.

Condemnation and Reactions

Father Montuclard's theses certainly did not correspond
to what all priest-workers were thinking. But they influenced many of them, and helped to discredit an experiment
which was opposed by all conservatives. In August 1953
the Vatican demanded the recall of the priest-workers and
the closing of the seminary of the *Mission de France* (a
certain number of seminarians had made designation as
priest-workers a condition of their ordination). These measures caused a great outcry, which extended far beyond
Catholic and labor groups; a religious question became a
national affair. Two of the many reactions to the liquida-
tion of the priest-workers are of special interest. One is a
letter from thirty-one priest-workers to the Archbishop of
Paris, Cardinal Feltin.

Paris, February 15, 1954
Your Eminence,
*The letter which has been communicated to us on behalf
of those bishops having priest-workers under their jurisdic-
tion has made us think seriously.*

*This document, in which you declare your total unity of
opinion with the Sovereign Pontiff, endeavored to remain
on the level of discipline, apart from questions of doctrine.
You know indeed, from your relations with us, that we
have always recognized your episcopal authority, that we
have never placed Christ or his Gospel in opposition to the
hierarchical Church, that we have always professed the
integrity of the Catholic faith, and that, with the help of
God, in this faith we live.*

*Nevertheless, the admiration and the gratitude that have
been lavished on us cannot blind anyone to the disavowal
of which we are the object, nor to the suspicion which falls*

upon our priesthood. In the eyes of public opinion, we are accused of betraying our duties and of denying to the working world that which it was our mission to bring to it. It is the honor of our priesthood, our dignity as men, which, in the name of the faith and obedience, are not being respected. We suffer therefrom on our own account. We suffer therefrom on behalf of our comrades whose essential aspirations the Church once again shows herself incapable of entertaining.

What the "Mission" was at its outset, several of its members, even its friends, who lived through those memorable days at Lisieux, can testify. Each one was aware of being faced with a decision that was to turn lives upside down. What demands the Mission would make, or how far it would lead, no one knew. But less than four years later Cardinal Suhard drew the moral when he stated publicly, "The Christian does not select his method. His mode of action is imposed on him by the environment into which he is plunged."

Hence the lengthy discussions in his presence of the "freedoms," as they were called, that were indispensable and without which it was no use setting out. In the end, three points survived:

(a) release from all parochial duty;

(b) this to include release from premature administration of the sacraments, experience having demonstrated that, among the ordinary people, this was often an obstacle to the sacramental system;

(c) liberty to live the full life of the proletariat (to the point of sharing its work, should that become clearly necessary).

The grant of these freedoms caused astonishment. Christian workers, trained by Catholic Action, saw in them a form of competition in their own particular field. Without waiting for what has now happened, they charged the priests of the Mission with neglecting the priestly functions for which they had been ordained and whose performance the priest-workers owed to them. Freedoms and objections alike had been accepted by Cardinal Suhard, when he received into his hands the promise of each of his priests "to consecrate his whole life to the Christianizing of the working class of Paris." He had merely stressed the serious and loyal spirit we were bound to bring to our team life. And that was the spirit in which other priests came to join the original small group. Our bishop had accepted responsibility for our undertaking and our development. Our promises were as much his as ours, and bound him as much as they did us. We were sent "not to baptize but to preach the gospel" (I Cor. 1:17), in a world that needed—not a priesthood different from that of our Church—but a priesthood different from the one it knew. So at that time our setting forth was encouraged on all sides.

Like Job accused by his friends, we will not allow anything to make us keep silence. No, we have not failed our promises. We have not defrauded our comrades of life, of the life indwelling in us. Our life, more than our words, bore witness from one day to another to Christ and his Church. Outsiders may have considered us as saying too little: our comrades made no mistake on that score. During those years there was much talk of "naturalization," of entering a world foreign to the Church. We have described its conditions as they were imposed on us, a little more each day, by the realities of working-class life. Even at Rome— where this development was closely watched—it was not considered then that those conditions were incompatible with our priesthood or with the faith of the Church. And now, abruptly, we are asked for what amounts to a recantation. How can we avoid feeling that we have been betrayed

and deceived? A growing tree plunges deep into the earth,
and the loving gardener respects its roots. For reasons all
of which have not been made known to us (as you yourself
recently said) and some of which are literally foreign to us,
we feel we are in large measure being sacrificed to the
demands of a plan of defense that will immobilize the
Church more than ever, turn her in on herself and bring
about for her that future she seeks to avoid.

The conditions imposed on us are far harder than anything we might have expected from our conversations with
you. We are being treated as guilty parties and threatened
with the harshest and most specific penalties. The roots we
have grown are being so little regarded that reduction to
the status of laymen is refused even to those who might
have thought of it. No heed is paid to the support and the
ever more exigent control we have mutually afforded ourselves. Instead we are required to join ecclesiastical communities, though it has been proved, every time these have
been tried, how limited and how risky they are. We are
forbidden to pool our own particular problems, while
Catholic Action is strengthening its national organs and
increasing the number of conferences of priests it arranges.
Why bring up the intolerable situation that would be created in their own small town or village for the relatives of
many of our number? Why put up the supposition of a
"revolt" when all our relations with you invalidate it? Is it
possible that the Church has forgotten the inner tragedy of
those of her children whom, throughout the painful conflicts that mark her history, she has disavowed, punished,
even imprisoned, and later taken credit for? Why speak of
sparing us the difficulties encountered by "those whose
weakness has led them astray," when it is well known that
our mutual union, had it been encouraged instead of being

curbed, would have rendered more difficult, perhaps prevented altogether, such rare "defections"?

No, your Eminence, it is not our priesthood that is being defended. Every year, without the Church being sufficiently alarmed to seek out the underlying reasons, priests desert their posts and their dioceses in order to get away from the disillusion and the scandal of a life too far from the ideal they caught a glimpse of in their youth; while others grow numb in a round of conscientious routine or struggle hopelessly in the meshes of a machine in which their initiative is broken on barriers they cannot surmount. That is something we are bound to say, in the name of all those who trusted us because we represented a light in their darkness, in the name of those who doubt whether their agony will ever be heard. We are bound to say it in the name of all the young men whose vocations are being discouraged at a time when the complaint is that there are too few of them, young men whose generous hearts are put at the mercy of an unconditional Promitto, or whose progress toward the priesthood is being halted because they ask to share the lot of the workers.

First and foremost, it seems, what needs defense is an ecclesiastical framework outside which neither faith nor priesthood are conceivably possible, and into which even unbelievers must fit or perish. Our mission was precisely to make good the inevitable narrowness of that framework into which it is desired to force us back, because religious authority today thinks it more valuable to strengthen its own hold than to ensure that the Church be present in the midst of the most burning problems of our times. The government and the circles supporting it justify their policy by saying that there are at present needs more urgent than relieving the misery that goes on growing. Ten years have passed since France, pays de mission? was published. What do certain religious circles still think? Want moves them to pity when it is defenseless. But they are disquieted when they see it preferring the organizations of its own making to the ones they promote. The consciousness and strength resulting from those organizations seem to them a more dangerous menace than the plight of the faith at which so much alarm was then taken in the name of missionary requirements. They recall that France is an ancient country of Christendom. With the surrounding countries, her duty is to become a bastion of the faith, in the face of the countries where the "Church of silence" patiently suffers.

There are wheels within wheels within wheels. Before God who is your judge, your Eminence, you declare that in all this affair there is no question of politics. Well, that is not our way of thinking. Things are infinitely more complicated. But, before God who is our judge, we declare to you that you are abolishing the true conditions of the mission and asking us to subscribe to their abolition. And we know that, if you did not feel such to be the case, the pain you suffer at this moment—as do many other bishops—would not be so great.

You ask us to empty the Gospel of participation in the harsh daily life of men. You want us to be satisfied with talking about it while we practice the virtues that have made the French clergy one of the foremost of the world: but they are virtues in which a whole people is honestly no longer able to find its own reflection. You even ask us for an inward submission to the measures taken against us without telling us how deep and how far may go the change of direction they require. You ask us in practice to forget the religious problems that have weighed us down and which can only be experienced within the working class.

There is a preliminary illusion that we must dispel. The bishops say to us, "Now that the workers love you and have realized, through you, that the Church loves them, your mission as priest-workers has become pointless: such close contact is no longer necessary." The workers have longer memories, and more experience. It is by our actions that they look to us and to you.

By our decision we shall be judged in the minds of the workers. Our decision will give its meaning to the years that have just come to an end. But already, by recalling us, the Church has given new life to a scandal whose weight is too heavy and comes too near home. What in your language you call temporal commitments are for our comrades commitments we undertook, with your consent, to the working class. For reasons the workers cannot understand, you have denounced them unilaterally, and you ask us to denounce them. That is something the workers are not likely to forget.

There is a second illusion. The Christian laymen whose way of life we share will not take our place. From the religious point of view their position will simply have become more difficult; for some of them it will have become untenable. These latter exist, and there are many of them. Yet it seems you do not wish to recognize them. They are even more numerous, and more worthy in the eyes of our unbelieving comrades, than those for the sake of whose faith you fear we may not submit.

We know that the novelty of the problems raised by our way of life and by our religious investigations has caused a lack of comprehension and a series of misunderstandings between the bishops and ourselves whose gravity we do not underrate. Certain quarters are beginning to bring against us the tendentious charge of having refused discussion with the hierarchy. You know, Eminence, that we have always regarded you as our bishop, and that we have always shown ourselves ready—particularly during the past six

months—to talk to you about our religious life and its conditions, about our concerns and your concerns. You know
that you promised to hold such talks with us, but you preferred to postpone what would clearly be a lengthy task,
while you limited yourself to public expression of your anxieties when the occasion seemed opportune. We loyally
admitted in your presence that adjustments were necessary,
and that was the point at which you chose to keep us at
arm's length, only to confront us with a fait accompli.

We have been told that a mission means setting forth
without possibility of return and necessarily means making
a break—with the past, with a particular training, mentality, culture and sociological environment, even to the
point of being able to burn one's boats. We believed in
what we were asked for, and have lived accordingly. We do
not ask you to live the life you have asked of us—a request
not at all surprising coming from the successor of the Apostles. We do ask you to respect the roots we have grown. We
do ask you not to stifle in us Christ's call to share the lot of
our brethren in labor. We ask you to respect the tension
that has arisen in us and in others between the working-
class conscience and our faith in Christ and his Church. We
ask you not to betray the missionary endeavor of France in
the name of higher interests.

Two years before his death, your predecessor wrote,
"This mission must succeed—here and now, because a
check at the outset would put the problem off indefinitely
to a time when the opportunities now open will not return;
and also, I admit, because the mission has, in my unworthy
person and the support I afford it, a means of growth it
might not find again." We feel bound to ask you, your
Eminence, whether today Cardinal Suhard would not be
disavowed, even condemned.

We have addressed ourselves to you, whether secular

clergy or members of religious orders, and wherever our canonical obedience lies, as being the leader of the apostolate and the mission in the diocese of Paris. The working class is one. As a group we were given a mission to it. We had to tell you as a group what as a group we have during these years discovered, brought to fruition and suffered. We have too much respect for each other for any of those pressures or tensions you seem to fear to exist between us at this time of sorrow. It is in entire freedom and entire liberty that each individual now faces your decisions. But as a group, your Eminence, we are bound to tell you that the choice you set before us is an impossible one.

There is a final point on which we all agree. What we have tried to say to you must not remain hidden from those Christians—workers or not—who are so deeply troubled at this time, and who are only too likely to interpret loyalty to the working class as disloyalty to the Church. It would be unnatural and painful for us and for thousands of Christians if this statement of our quest and our faith were not as clearly known as the devotion we have displayed for our worker comrades.[13]

Another reaction to the suppression came from one of the most eminent theologians of the Dominican order, Father M. D. Chenu, whose reflection went beyond the particular experiment of the priest-workers and considered the problem of the priesthood as a whole:

Since the existence of the priest-workers has been questioned, the problems caused by their missionary experiment in the Church have come to light, helping us to reflect on their priesthood, which is the most important question. Individually and collectively, they have laid bare their own

serious thinking on this subject; it merits a calm evaluation,
without emotionalism or equivocal concessions.

The essential functions of the priesthood are conceived
as the adoration of prayer, the celebration of Mass, the
administration of the sacraments, and catechetical and pastoral teaching. From this standpoint, obviously, the priest-
workers must seem to be exercising a diminished priesthood, since they are not in charge of an established Christian
community and they are not constantly performing these
functions. Such an amputation would then seem tolerable
only in grievous circumstances, because of which we might
regretfully consent to a doctrinally and apostolically ab-
normal situation. . . .

If this is so, the priest-workers will have to resign themselves to a blow which wounds their apostolic conviction,
and consent to their diminished situation as an effect of the
Church's loss of authority among the workers. But we believe that a more complete theology of the priesthood
would offer a different view of the problem. . . .

When a geographically and socially constituted human
group exists outside the faith and mystery of Christ, the first
duty of the priesthood is to carry the witness of faith and
the mystery of Christ to this non-Christian world. The sacramental initiation will be made only in the interior of this
testimony. Faith is not an easily presupposed, simple and
preliminary condition, but the very substance of the apostolic message, and its first act. The first function of the
priesthood is thus to give men the Word of God where they
can hear it, right where they are.

Recent works, like those of Father Rétif in France, have
given great emphasis to this first act of evangelization.
Whether it is a question of the primitive Church or of
pontifical directives, the evangelical message is first presented as the shock of the kerygma—the proclamation by

the public crier. Its value to the non-Christian is important, before there is any question of organized catechetics, or the sacraments. A Church that is well organized and planted in human society naturally sees the role and extent of the kerygma as reduced. But periodically, when the Church is faced with new and non-baptized worlds, this proper function reappears, without lessening the role of the sacrament which, as soon as possible, will fully realize the mystery of Christ, received in faith.

The phrase of Cardinal Suhard springs to mind here, which for ten years has expressed the extreme apostolic sensibility to such a situation in the new world: the Church is in a "missionary state." It is inevitable that a Church that has become comfortable in a well-ordered Christendom would be surprised by this new "state," but it offers hope to the apostle who wishes to give the witness of Christ to a new world, just as the primitive Church was seized by the Spirit to carry the evangelical message to the Gentiles. This missionary act cannot be seen as a marginal function for the priest, as if it were a simple preliminary episode.

It is obvious that, apart from the case of the priest-workers, reservations and suspicions are being expressed about a missionary status for the priesthood. The Mission de France has been led to underline the primacy of evangelization over other functions of the priesthood—certainly not treating them as secondary, but in order to carry the message of the Gospel to non-Christians, which may eventually lead them to the sacraments. The missionary is, precisely, the man who addresses himself to the non-Christian.

It is understandable that in the face of such a strong apostolic appeal a theology of the priesthood should feel the need for a better balance of the complex and complementary truths of Revelation within the role of the priesthood. The priestly spirituality we grew up with was constructed from the vantage point of an established Christian ministry. It was inevitable that the first function of the message to non-Christians would thus be blurred to the benefit of the particular functions of the "Levite." In his 1949 pastoral letter, Cardinal Suhard said:

The priest's role, always the same in its essence, can take on, and in fact has in past ages, a variety of expressions and functions, to emphasize especially its regal character, or its power of prophecy, or its acts of worship. . . . The priest's missionary task . . . will not consist in the beginning of baptizing individuals but, in accordance with an often-quoted formula, in "planting the Church" right in the heart of the masses, in every social sphere.

Such a program presupposes an immense effort. In the first place, a mental effort. The Christianization of this new world calls for a real work of intellectual abnegation. It may take a long time to break away from certain "methods suited to medieval Christianity." We have, and shall have, much hardship in breaking with a pattern which very legitimately for its own time was worked out by a theology which could only draw its inductions from a Christian state of affairs. So the most profound theological bases of the idea of the priesthood have to be re-examined and a new pattern of spirituality for priests worked out, through analysis and synthesis.[14]

The time for this is now.

The priesthood is not defined only by its function of sacramentally continuing the Mystery of Christ in established Christian communities, but is "missionary," and has the function and mission of evangelizing the Gentiles. . . . If we understand the primary demands of faith, and the witness of Christ's Church in the world in these terms, we will be better able to measure the dimensions of the Church itself. Obviously, we are going in opposition to the theology of the handbooks, which, in order to meet the needs of the

Counter Reformation, insisted on the sacramental apparatus in the face of a heresy which placed faith in opposition to it. . . . We are rediscovering the totality of an ecclesiology once taught by the Fathers and the great teachers of the thirteenth century. The debate over the priest-workers is only one special aspect of a doctrinal elaboration of the different roles in the Mystical Body of Christ. . . .

The virtues of faith, hope and charity exercise a theological primacy with respect to the moral virtue of religion, whose acts are elevated to the perspective of the Kingdom announced by Christ. Faith and its witness are not so much obligatory because of a precept; they are necessary only insofar as they are the principle of life and the law of the Gospel (St. Thomas, Ia, IIae, q.100, a4, ad1). In this technical formulation of the theologian, we can locate the major emphasis of the present missionary movement, and it is this which is under attack.

There remains the concrete problem of the commitment of certain priests to the life of workers; this reminds us not so much of the apostasy of the working class, but of its birth and formation completely apart from Christianity. The Church is literally a stranger to the workers' world.

This is not the place to treat this point, but it is evident that the doctrinal perspectives we have mentioned authorize the apostolic and sacerdotal truth of this ministry among the workers. Whatever regulations may need to be established regarding their status, it seems that this ministry is governed by a basic (and very difficult) act of presence, in the strong meaning we give this word today—a presence of the Church, which only a sharing of life and conditions makes real. How can we baptize a civilization if we do not enter it?

This presence is certainly not yet a "teaching" (didaché), nor a sacrament. But it is a necessary condition before a word may be spoken, including the Word of God. In the full force of the term, (and the popular stir resulting from the priest-worker dispute proves it), it is an efficacious testimony of faith. It is the first expression, in act, if not always in words, of a true evangelization, and thus of the visible face of the Church.

The unavoidable conditions of such a presence, above the walls of separation, are to be observed and measured. But if one gives the priesthood its primary dimensions, these conditions, which have been posed by the hierarchy, will no longer appear as distressing and regrettable concessions but rather as a guarantee of the presence of the Spirit in the Church and as a Christian hope for a world in preparation.[15]

With the tacit agreement of several bishops, the priest-workers continued here and there, but in September 1959 a letter from the Holy Office signed by Cardinal Pizzardo demanded the recall of some sixty priests still at work. The experiment of the priest-workers ended unhappily, with keen disappointment and even bitterness. In time the social and intellectual climate of France began to change, and the condition of the workers gradually improved. But didn't the priest-worker experiment have a larger dimension than the situation in which it was born? Was it not a significant witness with a profound meaning for many different situations, an invitation to become again a missionary and truly universal Church? It is in these terms that, as early as 1954, a great Catholic economist, François Perroux, interpreted the events:

The effort of those French Catholics who are now being tested marks a stage in a great work which was begun long ago. Catholic Christians in France have undertaken a relentless uprooting of eternal values from their eminently perishable political and economic settings. This attempt necessarily puts them in conflict with certain acquired rights and accepted situations. Once we have understood that, we know that the movement will be fought, but we doubt that it can be stopped; it is nourished by a sharp sense of reality and reactions written deep in the Gospels.

We must construct a society which does not refuse any human being the practical, concrete and immediate conditions of liberty, or the possibility of his participation in the highest values. Everyone is agreed, you will say. If this were really so, the climate of the struggle and the tone of the argument would not be what they are; some people obviously consider the temporal conditions of our universal ideal as irrelevant and superfluous. The idea of priests entering factories and workshops is a novelty which disturbs and disquiets them. . . .

But the deep reactions which the Gospel produces and inspires will always remove the Christian from the deception inevitable in all established orders, and will throw him on the side of the workers, the humble, and the suffering. It is almost banal to repeat it, yet we are obliged to. The excuse for repeating this primary truth is that in these times it seems unwise to do so.

The intimate contact of the priesthood and labor can no longer be effaced from history. Those among us whose profession is to interpret social realities are discovering in this contact an experience with decisive implications and a density of profound meaning.

Industrial progress has not succeeded in eliminating the labor of the individual who makes it possible. It tends to make men's painful efforts simply an object to be bought. It pretends to improve the conditions of work, all the while reducing it to a mechanical activity. Workers are beginning

to rebel. They think their work has a human meaning.
They declare, and prove, that it is a means of liberating a
class, and along with this class, all of humanity. It is very
simple, it is irresistible. We would be wise to appreciate this
attitude and furnish the best opportunities for this liberation.

We are faced with a choice:

Either a work which one learns and submits to, which is
sold and fought over like a thing exchanged in an unequal
contract;

Or a fully efficacious work, penetrated by the Spirit,
inspired and consecrated.

Consecrated—that is the essential word. This moment in
the evolution of human effort is the very one in which
French priests have decided to restore to the workers'
world the fullness of its human and evangelical meaning, in
their own persons and in the heart of the factory.

The celebration of such a mystery has traced a page
which can never be erased from the religious history of
mankind. It will be reread, and from it will come reaf-
firmed resolutions and further accomplishments.

Our societies are nourished by daring projects which are
immediately rejected in horror, then assimilated—at first,
timidly, in the end, completely. Our progress is made possible by activities which have become common through the
unwearying effort of innovators who persevered in the
midst of doubt and ridicule.[16]

III

Toward a Christian Realism

Immanence and Transcendence

The War and its aftermath taught French Catholics to distrust those who talked the most about "spiritual nobility." They saw that we do not enter the meaning of things or prepare the world for the reception of grace by pretending to stand apart from everyday realities. "Realism" is a much-abused term, but it can fairly be said that French Catholics have opted for a certain realism that long years of struggle against the "moderns" had made them forget.

The censorious immediately raised the cry: "They are choosing the Incarnation rather than the Redemption!"—a good example of their fear of complexity. But their fears had an object: French Catholics were becoming more and more anxious to mix the leaven of the Gospel in the dough of this world; would the lordship of Jesus be forgotten? The

89

experience of French Catholics shows, on the contrary, that the more the believer became involved in the earthy realities of everyday problems, the more necessary God's transcendence became to him. He loves the world too much to be satisfied with any outcome other than the salvation offered by God. There is no more opposition between the Incarnation and the Redemption than between Christmas and Easter, or work and glory.

Long before Teilhard, Maurice Blondel—whose influence on twentieth-century French Catholicism was decisive —had spent a lifetime studying the relations of faith and reason, nature and grace, as philosophical questions. For his pains (and for being ahead of his time), this firm Catholic was accused of Modernism. He took seriously the problems of his contemporaries, for whom "the notion of immanence is the very condition of philosophy. . . . Nothing can enter man which does not come from him and in some way correspond to his need of expansion."* But if religion is definitely "incompatible with the principle of immanence," people would conclude "that it is impossible to accept religion without renouncing reason, and that in particular it is impossible to be a Christian without denying man." Nevertheless, "to refuse to be divinized is to damn oneself," and "we can achieve our salvation only through grace, since, by definition, the supernatural is beyond our grasp." Blondel attempted to resolve this contradiction by showing that man's action postulates a supernatural conclusion without which he would fail to become fully man according to nature. "There is no contradiction between

* Maurice Blondel (1861–1949) was the author of l'Action. Quotations within the paragraph are taken from Lettre sur les exigences de la pensée contemporaine en matière d'apologetique (1896); it appears with another of his works in The Letter on Apologetics and History and Dogma, texts presented and edited by Alexander Dru and Illtyd Trethowan (New York: Holt, Rinehart and Winston, 1965).

being man and being Christian if it is shown that one cannot be a man if one refuses to be Christian," wrote Father de Montcheuil.

What Blondel dealt with as a philosopher has been taken up by others as men of action, artists, or theologians. If there was a greater awareness of the need for distinctions, the underlying purpose of these distinctions was intellectual unity, as the title of Maritain's major work, *Distinguir pour unir ou les degrés du savoir*, suggested.[1] Obviously, they are not new, but this statement of Father de Montcheuil shows that by 1942 the very notion of "Christian civilization" had become ambiguous, as the war and the Resistance had altered the relation of Christians to the nation:

Genuine civilization can only be Christian, since it is based on an idea of human nature which is kept intact only through Christian influence. This does not mean that civilization is the work of the Church; although the Church provides its ideal, there remains the task of discovering, within the concrete conditions of history, how human values will be expressed, realized, and defended. This is the work of men. For example, how is culture to be developed? How can it be made accessible to all those for whom it is a good? The Church does not tell us. Which are the institutions that, in a given stage of evolution, will provide the best realization of justice and unity? It is up to man to find out. . . .

Christianity is not the civilization, nor does it contain a ready-made plan for a civilization, but because of what it demands for man even in terms of his temporal destiny, it is the great civilizing force. When we study the history of Christian civilization we notice some of its effects, but its possibilities of realization are far from having been expressed, and even farther from having been exhausted. Our *task is to make it bear greater fruits in the future. Christian civilization always represents the future.*[2]

Father de Montcheuil belonged to the prewar generation, and was one of those who helped prepare young Catholics to confront a new political situation during the war. The Pétain regime made the Republic seem perfect by comparison, and young people in the Resistance believed in the imminent birth of a reasonable and just society in which Catholics would make their contribution, without any desire for special privileges.

Internal Controversy

In December 1945, the Association Catholique de la Jeunesse Française, which represented Catholic youth of every social class, held its first postwar convention. The address of its President, Alain Barrère, emphasized that for the ACJF, there was no such thing as an abstract city; it would "bear witness to its love for an incarnate city which has a name: France":

As an association of a wide variety of specialized movements, the ACJF is the representative body of French youth. It is not a simple youth group with its own interests, but a movement which exists for others, taking up the problems of the day that are of concern to all young people. What I am saying is that although our movement is fundamentally Christian, it is not a denominational group that simply brings together those who share a certain point of view; we exist for the service of all. In this we differ from various political youth groups, since our aim is not to impose a doctrine, but, by the transformation of our various milieux, to permit young people to have access to a more fully human life.[3]

As we see, the spirit of the ACJF reflected both its Christian concern and the ideas of Aristotle and of liberal democracy: man is a political animal who can and should use his reason to construct a society in which justice will be powerful and power just. This can take place only through representative government; the participation of individuals and groups is the one guarantee that the power of the state will not degenerate into pure violence. The ACJF leadership consisted of liberals within the structure of French Catholicism, and took democracy seriously; before the war, it should be remembered, the rightist *Action française* movement had been extremely influential, with its strange mixture of traditionalist Catholicism, and uncritical devotion to the state.

Naturally, the ACJF had its critics. For example, there were partisans of other ideologies—the *progressistes* (who often collaborated with Communists), the rightists (who defended French colonialism in Indochina and Algeria), and, later on, the Gaullistes (some of whom were ambiguous, or merely pragmatic in their support). In addition, the ACJF was attacked for theological reasons: the heart of the debate was the accusation that a Catholic Action group was being transformed into a political movement. In reality, young Catholics were trying to reach a better understanding of what the world meant to Jesus, of the mission of the Church and how it should be conducted. For several years, the hierarchy emphasized prudence, and limited itself to making neat distinctions—so clean-cut they seemed artificial to laymen working in the everyday world. It was said that the "temporal" should be sharply distinguished from the "spiritual," that "civilization" should not be confused with "evangelization," and that Catholic movements like the ACJF should keep somewhat apart from the concerns of the temporal order without completely ignoring it. Of course, these distinctions are not without meaning, but such an approach tends to keep the Church and the world in sealed and separate compartments. The heritage of the Counter Reformation is still in evidence. It was necessary that the collective experience of Christians should ripen, and that theology should reflect on that experience. Inevitably, new controversies and crises would constitute part of the learning process.

In 1956, André Vial, the President of the ACJF, who had been trained in the young farmers' branch of Catholic Action, turned in his resignation and issued a revealing statement:

> *I am resigning because the ACJF policy, which I accepted and wished to advance, is no longer supported by everyone. . . .*
> *I am resigning also because too many people seem to be afraid of a vigorous ACJF. The JOC is afraid that participation by their leaders and militants would turn them from their responsibilities to the working class. I have always believed, on the contrary, that the ACJF would be instrumental in preparing a more profound involvement within a given milieu. Some chaplains are afraid that a lively ACJF would mean the end of their intellectual paternalism. Many in the adult groups seem to look on the ACJF as a threat to their own recruitment. . . .*
> *In addition, I have been deeply affected by the attitude of some priests (including chaplains of our movements), who have employed methods that civil society would reject and which hardly seem in keeping with the spirit of the Gospel. . . . The primary reason for many of these attacks seems to be the resentment against the Jesuits, who have provided so many of our most successful chaplains. . . .*
> *Another major accusation against us is that we have be-*

*come political. . . . If there were need of it, I would swear
that during my ten years in Paris, the ACJF has never
followed any political direction. . . .*[4]

The problems were clearly analyzed: the ACJF disappeared (the final result of Vial's departure) because it was
accused of being more a political than a religious instrument, and of being dominated by Jesuits. The worker
leaders within played a separate game as well, accusing
the ACJF of not recognizing the originality of the
working class and of turning young workers away from
their responsibilities in their own field. On all these questions, however, history seems to have justified the ACJF
against its detractors. At the Council the Church made
clear that Christianity is not external to history; and in
France today it is no longer definite whether there is still a
genuine working class. At most, the ACJF could be criticized for having been too timid. When Vial justified the
ACJF in its task of training members to play a more informed role in their commitment to the world, he had to
use the traditional vocabulary of the Church. He did not
know how to define the link between faith and the world in
sufficiently positive terms, and thus unintentionally demonstrated the necessity of further theological reflection.

After his resignation, the Assembly of Cardinals and
Archbishops issued a statement and a doctrinal note which
recalled that "Catholic Action is an organized apostolate,
working in collaboration with the apostolic mission of the
hierarchy," and that the individual involvement of the laity
in temporal action is a duty:

*On the level of the movement itself, not simply of indi-
vidual action, it is normal that problems concerning the
young should be studied by all the movements. . . . In this*

study, if they wish to be faithful to the mission of Catholic
Action, they should seek together, over and above the important social and civic aspects of the problems, their
apostolic dimension—their repercussions in the Christian
life of the young and the obstacles they may offer to evangelization. In addition, the ACJF should co-ordinate its
efforts in those areas where the unity of young Catholics
can easily be achieved—for example, housing and social
charity, leisure and contemporary culture—with respect
for inevitable differences and their adaptation to a specialized milieu.

As the ACJF itself declares, youth movements ought to
halt their activity at the frontier of purely technical political problems, which are the domain of political parties, are
matters of free choice, and inevitably provoke opposition.
In his work for Catholic Action, the apostle cannot be a
partisan. . . .

The freedom of Christians, which the Church wishes to
protect in all areas of choice, would be menaced if the
ACJF, in the pursuit of a "politics for the young," became
involved in taking an official position on the basis of a
majority vote on questions that should remain open. This
would only make for divisions and quarrels within the
ACJF, which should be a center of unity for every son of
the Church.[5]

The prudence of the hierarchy was necessary, but with
the passage of time, who would not notice that some of its
statements bordered on nominalism? Perhaps nothing better could be done at the time, since the crisis persisted. On
May 9, 1957, the national leaders of *Route*, the oldest
branch of the Scout movement, turned in their resignation. This was the result of an interior conflict: *Route*
wanted to publish in its journal an invitation to read the

letters of a member, killed in Algeria, who had criticized various methods used in carrying on the war.* The board of directors of the Scout movement opposed publication, both for political and theological reasons, as in the case of the ACJF; they claimed that the letters were unfair to the French army and that their subject was outside the competence of a Catholic organization. The *Route* team issued a reply, with the following conclusion:

The difficulties of Route are not isolated; apparently, a certain kind of youth movement is still not accepted.

What are the fundamental aspirations of all these movements? A training in commitment which would make its members responsible adults, not aesthetes or "noble souls." A concern to examine political, economic, and social situations which will influence the next generation. A desire to form consciences, not by the manipulation of an abstract casuistry, but by relating principles to the most burning issues of the day.

Such an attitude will inevitably give offense, especially since it is generally accompanied by an indifference to the argument from authority.

The Algerian War, by sharpening the divisions among French Catholics to the highest point since the German Occupation, has shown the youth movements the obstacles that must still be surmounted. There was never a question that their leaders would remain silent during a conflict which administrative negligence, broken promises, poverty, and injustice had done so much to bring about.

None of these controversies shook the fidelity of French Catholics, but they discouraged many who were asking serious questions regarding the role of the layman in the

* See Chapter 6.

Church. There were no heresies or schism; but only a few years before the Council, many French Catholics would have confessed to a general sense of weariness. When the encyclical *Humani Generis* appeared in 1950, Henri Marrou had reminded the French Catholics that the generosity of Christians was no guarantee that they would not make mistakes, and that the faith of the Church should not be taken lightly by impatient innovators or supercilious integralists:

Many readers of the encyclical have been struck by the very elementary nature of the doctrinal exposition (obviously, the one-line definition of existentialism has no technical ambition); in its own terms, it only wishes to repeat certain well-known truths. What is under attack is not an original movement of thought so much as obvious deviations (often caricatured) that hasty popularization has engendered. We are in the paradoxical situation of having heresies without heresiarchs.

Far more than the thinkers whom we invoke, it is we who bear the responsibility for the errors that have been condemned. We should examine ourselves to see if, and to what degree, we have sinned through love of novelty, superficiality, and uninformed zealousness, and an insufficient understanding of doctrine. We must be honest enough to analyze our generation without flattery. Obsessed by problems of the practical order, pressed to move immediately to action, we have become almost indifferent to purely speculative knowledge, which has resulted in a lowering of theological understanding; the most fundamental principles on which the faith rests often appear to have been forgotten.

There seems an immense weariness in the voice of the Holy Father as he repeats once more those "well-known

truths" that the wisdom of the Church has so often had the
occasion to formulate and defend during twenty centuries
of history; the "new opinions" of 1950 are most often only
disinterments of very old problems. . . .

It is a truism worth recalling that the Catholic Church
cannot be conceived in separation from the doctrinal
elaboration it acquired over so many centuries; the work of
so many doctors of the Church, so many controversialists,
Councils, and Popes cannot have been in vain. This does
not mean, as some have pretended maliciously, that Catholics wish to enlarge the Trinity: Father, Son, Holy Spirit—
and St. Thomas! Regardless of the high place given to
Thomism, no one can pretend to identify it with the totality
of Christian thought; the most sincere Thomists are the first
to demonstrate, by the original contribution of their own
work, that St. Thomas can and ought to be clarified, completed, and, in a sense, transcended. But in the eyes of a
Catholic this can take place only by totally and authentically assuming its earlier intellectual tradition.

Obviously, it is not a question of turning every Catholic
into a theologian, but he should become aware of his faith
and nourish his understanding of it at the level of his own
culture. Faith is not inert but lives in the soul of the believer in such a way as to grow, or to die. It is not without
reason that the first sentence of the encyclical uses the term
—surprising in Latin—Christian culture; the Catholic faith
asks the believer to make a cultural effort (understanding
the word "culture" in the subjective sense), and this culture
is truly Catholic only if it is nourished by the authorized
source of the magisterium, for it is in the Church and by
the Church that we have access to the words of eternal
life. . . .

There are too many frightened spirits in Catholic circles
who cannot seem to understand that error—or, if one in-

sists, heresy—is an inevitable by-product of any creative doctrinal speculation (that the Pope should have to put the Church on guard against certain false opinions is, in one sense, a consoling sign; since people are in danger of deceiving themselves, they are at least thinking actively!). These people confuse orthodoxy and lazy-mindedness, doctrinal accuracy and the memorizing of formulas, and, in order to avoid error, are glad to give up thinking and would like others to do the same.

Such defenders of the faith are naturally inclined to retain merely the negative conclusions of the encyclical, and to draw from it negative rules of behavior as well; in their eyes every historian of dogma will be tainted with historicism from now on, anyone intent on praying ad tollendum schisma will be accused of "false irenicism," any study of the spiritual exegesis of the Fathers (even when as objectively conducted and as prudent in its conclusions as de Lubac's fine book on Origen [Histoire et Esprit, l'intelligence de l'écriture d'après Origen]) will be identified with the rapturous fantasies of Paul Claudel. We must exercise a special vigilance against such tendencies in the Church. I use the phrase deliberately; since the Modernist crisis, there has been a "Vigilance Committee" in every diocese, whose assignment is to hunt out heresy. It is indeed necessary to safeguard the purity of the faith, but the health of the Church equally requires that it be defended against stupidity.

An attentive rereading of Humani Generis should make it clear that the Holy Father is concerned to guard against such deviations ahead of time. With each of his warnings he takes care to specify that if there are errors to be avoided in a particular area, it does not follow that Catholic scholars should be told to give up the work they have begun. There is a warning against modern philosophies, but also a reminder that Catholic philosophers and theolo-

gians have the duty to be familiar with them, and that such
study may well be the occasion of considerable benefit,
either through the assimilation of their partial truth, or by
the deepening of traditional truths that their refutation will
require. If there is a criticism of doctrinal relativism, it is in
order to affirm the norms of the homogeneous and consistent progress of theology. If there is reference to a danger in
an exclusive reliance on the Bible and the Fathers, the return to the sources is proclaimed the constant duty of every
theologian, as long as it is carried on in the full light of the
explicit teachings of the magisterium. Indeed, we are for-
mally told that biblical and patristic studies are the means
by which the sacred sciences are constantly renewed, guar-
anteeing the fecundity of speculation.

Far from discouraging research endeavors, the document gives them encouragement, asking only for greater
rigor and precision in execution. It should be plain that this
encyclical, in which some have wished to find only ob-
scurantism and reaction, should constitute—if Catholic
thought knows how to respond to it with sincerity, intelligence, and vigor—a decisive stage in the unfolding of a
great age of theology.[6]

It is hard to say what one should admire more—the
rigor of Marrou's thought or his skill in demonstrating that
the encyclical should not be read in negative terms. Catholic scholars might use a somewhat different vocabulary
today, but it is now taken for granted that further research
is an obligation, in theology as in every other area.

Universal Science and an Economy for Man

Despite the slowdown occasioned by *Humani Generis*,
French Catholics continued, as Pope John would later
counsel, to read the signs of the time. If theological

questions seemed to be pursued with less vigor, this was
perhaps partly because of fatigue and a greater concern for
prudence; some of the best scholars underwent an ordeal
which may well have been purifying. The Church reminded
them, sometimes rudely, that the faithful Christian is bound
in solidarity with the people of God and the ecclesiastical
institution, the bearer of revelation and heir of tradition,
and that God is not to be misused. They were also tested
by the world's complexity and mobility, since its changes
required a constant questioning of prior certitudes. It is,
therefore, with an extra measure of respect and seriousness
that these Christians confronted the mystery of history.
They went on with their task; they denied neither their
faith nor history, but continued to hold on to both ends of
the chain.

For example, Father Dominique Dubarle, O.P., a specialist in the philosophy of science, analyzed the new challenge presented by the universality of science:

Etymologically, the adjective "catholic" means the desire of the faith to embrace the whole earth, to gather all
mankind together in principle, to welcome within its concrete synthesis the richness and plenitude of the created
world. This corresponds to an ideal of complete spiritual
integration, an ideal which science also proposes in its own
manner. Science, too, knows that it is destined to gather all
men together, and gradually to absorb the reality of things
within its universe of knowledge, by means of its capacity
for action and its social powers. Nevertheless, there is a
difference, which includes an important theological lesson.
The difference comes from the fact that science is in the
process of realizing its universal vocation to mankind, but
Catholicism is not. If we are to make a sober judgment of
its present historical condition, it can only be considered, at

least for the moment, as a particular religious confession along with others, Christian and non-Christian. . . .

Catholicism must therefore act as spokesman for a fraction of humanity, while working out a spiritually legitimate compromise between that which by natural vocation leads to historical universality (the gathering together of all humanity on a scientific level) and that which—although spiritual and even of the highest essence—will remain on this side of universality. To work out this compromise while fully respecting man, Catholicism should profit from the scientific event itself, remembering that the total universe of divine descent is present in a far less summary fashion than by its apparent belonging to a given religion or church. Part of its reality is in the process of quietly rooting itself in the human world. This has given Catholics human energies to which the faith has restored an élan, but the faith remains the act of the few.[7]

Reasoning as a theologian on the meaning of scientific universalism, Dubarle made some illuminating distinctions, which will be echoed with greater precision when the Council completes its work. For example, Father Congar, in a conference given at Rome during the third session, declared that only Christ exercises an absolute and universal lordship, that he alone is the principle, the Church being his servant. In this way one can take into account the limitations of the visible Church, the universality of the divine lordship which the Church must manifest to every creature, and the very positive value, in God's perspective, of the gathering together that is actually achieved through the ministry of reason.[8]

For François Perroux, there is no doubt that economics will one day be able to organize the entire planet in reasonable terms, and that the spirit of the Beatitudes, far from

being foreign to such an undertaking, ought to animate it.
Christians should use all their strength in hastening the
economic organization of the world. Not that economic
planning should be identified with salvation, but its effectiveness could alter the universal development of man. Of
course, this development must be completed by grace, but
we know that grace neither destroys nor replaces nature.

What kind of inner conversion could bring about an
uncompromising Christianity that would be taken seriously, be lived by every social class, and be capable of
leading nations away from killing and freeing economies
from avarice? Others, more authorized than I, have attempted to answer; my more modest domain is the secular
order.

In this area, science, honesty, and scientific rigor remain
the only guarantees of civilization. Of course, in reactionary circles the menaces of science are depicted without
showing its great liberating power. Apparently, it is necessary to repeat constantly that science, technology, and
complete rationality are essentially liberating. Humanity
does not suffer from knowing too much but too little. Men
are not in pain because they are too powerful, but because
they are impotent. There is no teaching or application of
science which does not offer the promise of liberty. People
should not try to frighten us with talk about "the end of the
world" for which science would be to blame. If the world
came to an end through miscalculation in a laboratory
oriented to liberty and life, this would be an end more
worthy of man than the slow freezing of the planet; human
civilization would have disappeared according to man's
law, at the zenith of his passion to know and conquer freedom.

Some will ask if the general public can understand or

accept this truth. But today the worker, just as much as the
member of an elite, can realize that the real task of humanity is to reveal, by the use of reason, the full value of the
entire planet, including all its latent resources, and all the
men who people it. Men have shown tireless courage and
endured frightful suffering so that we in the twentieth century might be able to attempt such an undertaking. . . . The
World Development Plan, which was ridiculed a few years
ago, is mentioned today in major declarations by every
chief of state; these men, who are at the summit of power,
see clearly that it is the only plan which might halt the
waste of human resources and put an end to war. . . .

Because such a project has nothing to do with profits,
and is in opposition to military solutions, it has been attacked by barbarians of every camp: its acceptance will be
the touchstone of our understanding of civilization. Surely
it is in agreement with the message of the Gospel. Only
when we have drowned out the blasphemous cries of
"Honor to the rich and powerful" will we be able to repeat
those lessons of purity and tenderness which were taught in
the Sermon on the Mount, and humbly ask Christ for the
great secret of the Beatitudes.[9]

The Lesson of Emmaüs

While some were writing and debating on the emerging
issues within French Catholicism and its relationship to the
world, others were beginning to realize specific initiatives
which grew out of the profoundest involvement with day-to-
day problems.

The career of Abbé Pierre is a good example. A priest
from Grenoble who organized one of the first Resistance
units, he was elected to the Assembly after the war as a
deputy for the Christian Democratic party, the Mouvement

republican populaire (MRP). He later broke with the party and worked with the poor in the suburbs of Paris. He founded a community of ragpickers, and taught them to support themselves by making intelligent use of garbage. After encountering thousands of families living without decent housing, he tried to help them by forming the Communauté d'Emmaüs. On January 4, 1954, after the French Assembly had adjourned without passing a bill that would create emergency housing, a baby froze to death in one of Abbé Pierre's cabins. On January 31 he appealed to the Christian conscience of France in a moving sermon, and the following day went on the national radio to issue a cry of distress: "My friends, help! A woman has just frozen to death on the sidewalk of Sébastopol Boulevard; she was still carrying her eviction notice." There was a spontaneous "explosion of goodness"; hundreds of thousands of people brought clothing, money, jewels. The government was startled into action, and the housing program was accelerated. The Communauté d'Emmaüs, however, continued to live among the poor, and extended its activities to the struggle against world underdevelopment. Ten years later, Abbé Pierre summarized the lesson of this experience:

The greatest problem today is to see to it (in a permanent manner, and not by police methods) that the privileged of this world and the whole human community wrench themselves free from the evil influences of their useless pretensions.

The most powerful means of saving the human family from this split between those who have the means and no longer know how, and those who know what is needed (they are dying of it) but have no power (they are often so exhausted that they cannot succeed in expressing themselves), is a kind of folly. Only an excess can counter-

balance an excess. Reason has its place only after a counterweight has re-established the equilibrium of things.

After so much criminal abdication has created such desperate conditions, it is not enough for those who have power to make the magnanimous decision to "serve." Many sons of "successful" families must have the wise folly to return to suffer, for long enough that it be genuine, with those who have been abandoned and are without resources. . . .

Just ten years ago there suddenly broke out what people called an "insurrection of goodness," an event which neither logic nor sociology can adequately explain because it occurred at the level of what, for the lack of a better word, is called "mysticism." Indeed, those who suddenly found themselves the instruments of this event were the most unprepared of all. Such an occurrence shows that the greatest force for the salvation of a society is in the challenge of love, which is born through the witness of the poor, who are "saved by becoming saviors."

But it seems that no one has revealed the most exceptional aspect of those days, that seed which was in such danger of perishing under the shock of the event. During those weeks when 300,000 letters arrived, bringing hundreds of thousands of francs to the poor ragpickers, they never ceased for even one day from making daily collections which would earn them a few thousand francs' worth of bottles, papers, and rags.

Of course, these men had faults; a number of them were heavy drinkers. But they continued to do their work, which was their "reason for living," to take pains in order to be able to give. "It's important," they insisted, "because this little bit that we do may be the tiny detonator which explodes the shell." What was magnificent was that something marvelous was accomplished by men who were not marvelous, simply because they had rediscovered—and had busied themselves to apply—that universal truth: "We should serve ahead of ourselves those who suffer more than ourselves". . . .

Since then there have been other Emmaüs communities springing up on every continent, each saving men and women who have been bruised by life, jarring the consciences of the comfortable, informing public opinion, and advancing the cause of the law of love, which does not mean simply "to serve," but also "to participate," since to love is to be with.

The certitudes which experience brings us are fine and strong, but they cost dearly; this is because they make us see how weak our effort is to respond to them with genuine acts, and because through them we are brought to face sufferings that are all but unbearable.

Nevertheless, these certitudes alone are worth the pain of living. In the communion of man, they represent even more than earthly peace, because they are a foretaste, in our poor souls, of the Eternal who is Love.[10]

French Catholics have not ceased to confront the realities of every day, and since this effort involves a bitter struggle, they have left some casualties on the field. Sacred history—which is linked to secular history—is not child's play. "Enter still further into the denseness," wrote John of the Cross, who is often thought to have lived outside the world. We do not pretend that the Catholic shock troops of recent years have all been like him; we simply observe that they have held together the different threads of their life. At the very moment when they plunged into the density of reality they turned toward God in order to know him and adore him. For the all-high God is also the hidden God, and the Prince of Nations is called Emmanuel.

IV

The Church Apostolic

Liturgy and Religious Education

Apostolic Church: These words designate both the early Church and the Church of every age when it fulfills its mission honestly. Confronted with today's staggering missionary responsibilities, French Catholics, like many others, turned to the origins of the Church as they tried to bear witness to God. French Catholicism since World War II—in its approach to the interior life, the liturgy, the organization of the Church, religious education, pastoral practice, or the problem of a contemporary religious art—has developed an apostolic flavor, emphasizing the neglected truth that the Church exists by itself but not for itself.

Parish life provides an instructive index. For centuries, the parish had been the community formed by the inhabitants of a village or a neighborhood, who assembled

around their church. Today, however, the parish church is
no longer the center of social life; believers are a minority,
and many have not remained in their villages. There are
those who believe that the parish no longer has a role to
play. Others regard it as the eucharistic community of believers, not the institution devoted to summoning unbelievers; it participates in the mission of the Church but is not
missionary in itself, since it is an established Christian
community. There were some parish priests, however, for
whom the community of believers could not be a closed
entity, who felt that a genuinely missionary effort would
create eucharistic communities. What was important was to
find out which language, organization, and basic approach
was best suited to the parish in a Church conscious of its
mission. These priests have tried to co-ordinate parish and
mission, and have sometimes succeeded in transforming
their parishes, awakening the faith of their members and
preparing them to welcome unbelievers and seek out opportunities to serve the total community.

Father Michonneau, a pastor in the working-class suburbs of Paris, was the first to speak of "the parish as a
missionary community." In 1945 he gave a first account of
his experience, in a book dedicated to Father Godin.

It is easy to pick out the great themes of Michonneau's
call for parish reform: a "living and missionary" liturgy;
renewal of the apostolate and prudent criticism of existing
parish organizations; keeping religion from looking like a
business enterprise; forming co-operative teams of priests;
avoiding linking the apostolate with middle-class culture;
inspiring Christians to stand out clearly, but without affec-
tation, among their fellows. He described the missionary
parish as a Christian community which does not foolishly
live within a citadel:

WHAT DO YOU MEAN WHEN YOU SAY "THE PARISH"? . . .

The first meaning. For some (and inasmuch as most of us do not react against routine, we usually fall into this category) the parish means the sum total of all those who come to church. "My parishioners," a priest will say. In this sum total we can distinguish several groups: first of all, the few really faithful ones who receive Communion every day or every Sunday, and who are the backbone of all parish activity; then, those who come to Mass every Sunday and whom the priest knows at least slightly; next, those who come to church for the big feasts, if only to offer their pious mite of worship, because, as they will tell you, they are "on the Church's side"; lastly, the borderline group of those who, in a sense, are well-disposed to religion, who have their children baptized and instructed for First Communion, who come to the church to be married (usually), who call for a priest at their deathbeds, and who hold to church burial as to a family custom.

According to this conception the parish means all those who have some contact with the church, with whom the priest has some connection—even if these relationships show a great similarity to commercial ones of some special nature.

Parish life becomes the cultural life of souls such as these. . . .

The clergy—pastor and curates—must divide their time between ministering to these souls according to their spiritual needs and taking care of temporal affairs. And this latter becomes more and more burdensome according to the number of the activities and according to the prosperity and growth of the parish.

Hence this concept means that "parish" and the parish milieu are identical. . . .

In our suburban parishes, even more than in the rural

areas, you will find the very essence of this parish spirit
spoken of above. Parish life here, more than in any other
place, is reduced to the ordinary life of this circle. The
smaller the proportion of this circle to the number of the
indifferent, the more is this noticeable. In the country,
those who come to church usually represent good people of
all classes. Here in the suburbs, since the pagan proletariat
is a tremendous majority, the contrast between parish life
and the life which goes on in this particular district is more
marked. A full church at Sunday Mass should not lull us
into thinking that all is well; let us look at realities.

It is easy enough for the clergy to be kept busy with the
faithful flock. The church will look full enough, and services and activities will be well attended. The priests will
think that they are reaching the masses because of the large
attendance, and they will think that they have here the real
reactions of the people; in reality they are reaching only the
"parish milieu." They will think they are succeeding because their ministry is bringing them satisfaction. In reality, they have no contact at all with the masses.

Another factor clouds our perspective. We tend to judge
the parish by the contacts we have in the church or sacristy,
with those who come about their children, or to arrange a
marriage. We are wrong. Those who come to see us—especially if they are ordinary folk—come with an attitude of
inferiority, even servility. They talk like us, but they do not
think like us. And the real hardened cases never come to
see us. How often, in our visits around the parish, we have
been conscious of that attitude of servility in families who
had a child in our catechism class. We could see it in their
very welcome. We realized that we were to make the decision whether or not their child should be admitted to his
First Communion; they were flattering us. They would not
dream of contradicting us in whatever we might say.

Besides all this, another enormous difficulty in parishes like ours is knowing our parishioners and remembering their names—let alone trying to look for them in church. And hence it is an easy step to begin to misconstrue their attitude, to make no effort to understand their mentality, and even to forget about those whom we no longer see around the church. Evangelization here is a terrible problem. It hurts us to think about those whom we must reach; forgetting about them is easier.

WHAT ABOUT THE OTHER MEANING OF A "PARISH"?

The other concept consists in this. Having studied a map of the parish, or—better still—after having made a walking tour of the whole place, we say to ourselves: Our parish is this entire territory; all those living inside this section are committed to our care, without any exception made because of nationality or immorality or hostility to the clergy. Nothing can free us from the obligation of caring for their souls. Hence all those who do not come to us, and whom we will never get to know unless we go to them; all those we meet—including Algerians and Chinese—they are all our parishioners. We have to say to ourselves, "We, their priests, have the care of these souls."[1]

Twenty years of experience only confirmed Michonneau in his initial intuitions:

The older I get, the more I insist that there is no ready-made formula for creating an apostolic, truly missionary parish. At the same time, I am more and more certain of the primacy, efficiency, and irreplaceability of the pastoral ministry. No parish can resist a united, open-minded team if it has made the effort to reflect and thought through the possibilities of adaptation. No parish will resist its evolution

into a living community; if we have faith in its future, the
parish will become missionary, and regardless of environment, can become part of the renewed Church.[2]

Of course, the liturgical movement began long before
the war, and was not of French origin. But in the forties,
French liturgists were generally pastors, and the pastors
often liturgists. One of the driving forces behind the movement was the aptly named *Centre de Pastorale liturgique.*
The Center represents the best in scholarship, but we are
far from the esoteric, decorative archaism which used to
afflict the liturgical movement. French Catholics suddenly
began to hunger for liturgical truth, at the very moment
that their missionary conscience was awakening. In a 1947
article in *La Maison-Dieu,* the Center's internationally
known journal, Father M. D. Chenu showed that liturgical
reform was not a task for experts alone. In the liturgy, the
grace of God "is expressed and transmitted by human acts
that have been ritualized for this purpose." Far from being
a collection of unintelligible practices which are to be observed passively, the liturgy of the Church takes human
behavior into account; it welcomes symbol and makes mystery manifest. Inspiration should not be destroyed by the
institution; the liturgy combines both. Father Chenu also
pointed out the relationship between liturgical participation
and contemporary mass civilization:

The economic interdependence among nations, the
widening of human activities due to the suppression of dis-
tances and the rapidity of exchanges, the concentration of
enterprises, the socialization of work, the organization of
professions, the ideological power of the news media and
propaganda, the vague feeling of coherence of a humanity
advancing in the midst of terrible tragedies—all these fac-

tors contribute to a mass civilization. Although we feel the heavy hand of such a civilization, we must not underrate its magnitude and its benefits, even spiritual ones. In any case, it raises the problem of the relationship between the person and the community—or better, the relationship of the diverse communities to which the person belongs.

This revolution of the community is refracted in Christian life, either because grace takes into consideration these human potentialities and new values, or because the community of the Mystical Body is seized by the same kind of aspiration. But renewal is apparent not only in the apostolic field of evangelization and parish administration, but also in the sacramental acts and their collective rites, the essential expression of the Christian community. The result is that, faced with the secular "liturgies" which mass ideologies and totalitarian regimes have brought to life, the Christian finds it necessary to canalize (so to speak) these communitarian instincts for the benefit of the salvation-community in which he lives. Today's liturgical renewal is developing in this atmosphere.

But the sociological parallelism which we observe shows immediately and at the same time the uniqueness of the Christian position and the difficulty encountered in trying to obtain the balance it requires. In Christianity the person is the subject of grace, in a love of God which, like any other love, is incommunicably personal, in a faith which is the supreme act of an inviolable freedom. Member of a mystical body whose head is Christ, the individual keeps his autonomy, carries his own sins and his own merits, speaks to God secretly, and, however severe the trial, continues to believe and love. This is the opposite of depersonalization and of the domination of collective instincts, no matter how pious they may be.

Nevertheless, this religious exaltation of the person is

fulfilled only in the rhythm of the community, its over-all order and blending of elements; we are not referring simply to the mysterious community of the Body of Christ but to the fraternal community which expresses it. It is there that the ordinary Christian people, the first clients of the Gospel, find the necessary resources for their life and discover the communal quality of the sacrament. They feel a great need to partake actively in the sacrificial meal, to understand baptism as an entry into a community, and to renew the practice of public confession in the manner of early Christians. The testimony of the lay people of the Paris Mission is revealing in this regard, and we are extremely impressed to see the most advanced pastors protesting set patterns and promoting new liturgical forms. There cannot be any better sign of Christian health. The community is the necessary locus of Christian life, necessary for the growth of individuals in both grace and character.

The liturgy will be renewed, therefore, to the degree that true communities are revived. The whole sociology of the community works in this sacred realm as well as on secular ground: its laws and techniques will have to be observed, beginning with the detection of natural communities (of neighborhood, of work, even of leisure) which will protect people from merely being part of a crowd and help spur an active liturgy. Pastoral liturgy has a great work ahead of it.[3]

Liturgical reform progressed without too much difficulty, but the reform of religious education was more laborious. Any revision of the catechesis* can seem to be calling the faith itself into question, but to refuse to adapt

---

* Catechesis, the basic instruction given to Christian catechumens preparing for baptism, was the standard term in the primitive Church and is used here in distinction from catechism, the term generally employed for a popular question-and-answer manual of doctrine. (Trans.)

this instruction to the men who receive it is to risk a withering of the faith. As French Catholics realized better their minority situation and the complexity of the world which had formed outside of them, they saw the necessity of revising the teaching of faith in order that it become eloquent without ceasing to be faithful. In the last decade, increasing numbers have attended the National Conference on Religious Education. In 1957 the religious education of children was described as a preparation for an adult faith, a reverence before the mystery of God, a training for Christian commitment. As Abbé Daniel, co-author of the famous *France, pays de mission?* said: "It is necessary to show, in the catechism and in the catechesis, not 'a something' but 'a someone,' and a someone very much alive." Catechesis, catechism: all religious education is taken into consideration, whether aimed at children or adults.

The French were developing an idea in which the Germans had been pioneers long before the Second World War. The imperfection of a teaching system based on a moralizing and intellectualist theology had long been recognized. By 1956, it had become possible to combine the discoveries of pedagogy, psychology, and sociology with the rich insights of the biblical and liturgical movements which had revived the Christian community. Naturally, it was no easy task to synthesize all this material. *Informations catholiques internationales* (No. 58, October 15, 1957) listed twenty possible errors to be avoided, including: breaking up the mystery of faith, which is at the same time doctrine, history, and mysticism; yielding to intellectualism under the pretext of enriching the intellect; altering the object of the teaching, which is God, with the excuse of adapting ourselves to different ages and temperaments; falling into a naïve belief regarding the freedom of the child; and using communication techniques improperly.

Because the task was important and difficult, self-appointed censors began to complain; finally Rome asked French bishops to give a warning. Those with appointed roles in the movement (Abbé Coudreau, Director of the Institut supérieur catéchétique; Canon Colomb, Director of the Centre National catéchistique and Secretary of the Commission nationale de l'enseignement religieux, created by the bishops), resigned their functions. Some of their books were revised. To tell the truth, these limited revisions were not unjustified and the Bishops' statement of September 18, 1957, did not interrupt the reform of religious education.

The Renewal of Religious Art

As one becomes more familiar with French Catholics today, he is quickly aware that they are neither negative nor lukewarm. Wishing to explore the depths of their faith, they live in fidelity—and sometimes in pain—that unity which is the Christian mystery.

Recent developments in religious art are a good indication of this. Men like Father Couturier, Father Régamey, and Abbé Morel, along with Matisse, Manessier, Rouault, Le Corbusier and hundreds of others, who differed in age, style, and belief, have been the authors of a revival which began prior to the Second World War. But in developing an authentic contemporary art for the Church, things do not move quickly. The creator is alone. The Christian is usually reluctant to link his prayer with forms which are too new. Moreover, such art is only the outer cover of the liturgy. The renewal of sacred art follows the broad lines of liturgical reform, however; the more Catholics began to realize that the Church liturgy was their own liturgy, the more they rejected a conventional art.

Fortunately, the men who saw the importance of sacred art knew that new forms should not be hastily adopted;

they had no intention of imposing the dictatorship of the avant-garde. They were the artisans of a reconciliation, gradually training their fellow Christians to look with a fresh glance at new creations which were not intended to be models. Thanks to them, we have the "witness" church of the Assy plateau, which contains the admirable Christ by Germaine Richier, stained glass windows by Rouault, mosaics by Fernand Léger, and works by Matisse, Braque, Bonnard, and Lurcat; the church in Audincourt; the chapel in Vence; the church in Ronchamp; the convent of La Tourette; and the complete file of *Art Sacré*, the journal which best reflects this effort.

Both the sensibility and faith of these men were very demanding. A few statements of Father Couturier are suggestive: "We must be against baroque. . . . By going back to baroque we would be turning away from real life. It stands for facility, and the refusal to make a choice. Would the revival of baroque have anything in common with the efforts of the priest-workers or the JOC?" And again: "In art, anything which is not new is a lie; it is like using someone else's words to speak." Finally: "We can grow only by doing things which require self-sacrifice."[4] If these words show partisanship, it is that of a creator or a friend of creators.

Father Régamey analyzed the current modes of the sense of the sacred in these terms:

It is the transcendent that engenders the sacred in art. Therefore, Christian worship above all should be stamped with the character of mystery. This is in contrast to past centuries, which sought either to subject the holy to rational analysis or else to reduce it to the level of the commonplace by obscuring it with sentiment. In our time, as the faithful become more and more aware of the God of the Bible and of the Te Deum, they tend to lose interest both in theodicy and in saccharine devotions.

The liturgy (when properly celebrated) has once again become the sincerest expression of our feeling for the sacred. The antithesis between the Christian and the sacred rite, between the Christian and the community, can only disappear through that love which at once animates the liturgical celebration and the faithful. In this experience, still not too common in our time but growing more frequent, we realize that Christian transcendence is in infinite love.

We discover in this way one of the ambivalences of the sacred. The need for asceticism, for the stripping of self, is allied to a radiation of spiritual splendor. They are correlative factors, two aspects of the same thing. There is the little bare chapel with its small handful of people, in a silence which is in perfect accord with the simplicity of the vestments, and the one small window over the altar, or it may be the Cathedral of Chartres, with eight thousand young people taking part in a dialogue Mass; in either case there is the fullness of love. We need not think of the bare chapel as something Jansenist, and we need not think of liturgical splendor in terms of brocade and gilt and plush, orchestras and violins. Whether it be the sound of magnificent choirs and organs or a few voices in unison, the secret place of the heart is always opened to God's love.

In sacred art we find again the decisive experiences which contributed to the history of French Catholics in recent years. God is triumphant and yet dwells in the most interior depths of one's being; there is suffering as well as glory; personal destinies are fulfilled within a united community; there is a fundamental harmony with the cosmos, which is the temple of the Creator.

Everything save sin is either sacred or capable of becoming sacred. Every rigid system of Christian art which claims to have its own consistency, its own laws and outlook, inevitably formalizes the sacred. The same is true of all ritualism that is devoid of life and has become a sham. This is not really surprising, of course, since every sacred expression becomes ritualized, and sacred art has always involved (like any other application of art to a specific function) submission and recourse to conventions. The symbolism of Christian art needs a system and it must have its own laws. But the conventions governing the sacred must be genuine in three ways: first, these conventions must constitute a language as direct and as transparent as possible to express the things of God and to convey their full meaning; second, this language must be used sincerely by the best artists of the period; and third, it must be the sincere and habitual expression of the faith of Christian people.

If the conventions which we have recourse to in sacred art conform to this threefold standard of authenticity, we have no need to fear formalism; but if our conventions are adopted in a spirit of reaction, then we cannot expect them to be very fruitful. Nothing in Christianity can ever be fruitful unless it is done in the framework of our communion with mankind as it really is. We have to be on our guard against any sense of the sacred that prescribes a closed system of signs, divorced from the life of our age and condescending to the individual Christian as if it were the heavenly Jerusalem coming down. Every sacred work is something of an epiphany, a transfiguration and a parousia. But it is so only in terms of our present humble condition, in which we can do nothing of value for God if we are not in communion with each other. And what art is possible when we are as divided as we are today?[5]

Toward a Contemporary Spirituality

Father Perrin's insistence that the priest renew contact with human life provides good introduction for a portrait of the French priest. He is generally poor, humble, haunted by the fear of living in a vacuum, eager to offer a bread which would truly nourish his people. There remain some strait-laced priests pretending to be crusaders; one may also smile at some young priests who want to be up-to-date and outdo the most intemperate laymen in irresponsibility; when all is said, however, French priests deserve considerable praise. Bishops, too, are adopting a new style; the bishop-prince is fast disappearing. Because of this, many lay people are beginning to look with new interest at the interior life of the Church. The most-read inquiries in *Témoignage chrétien* were about the use of the vernacular in the liturgy, the place of money in the Church, First Communion, the role of the priest, and parish renewal.

A portrait of today's Catholic layman should also be drawn. But there is no one French layman, because French Catholicism is not uniform. Some may complain of individualism, but without it the spirit of invention and responsibility would not have flowered in the French Church at the same time that political society seemed to take away man's freedom.

Laymen educated by Catholic Action have shaken some ecclesiastical structures and intellectual systems that were linked with the idea of an omnipotent clergy and the humble position of ordinary Catholics. But the crisis of the ACJF did not prevent many lay people from finding their way without losing their faith. New groups of laymen have formed, hoping to become better acquainted with the Lord and also to serve man, and to avoid both clericalism and the political spirit. For example, the Little Brothers and the

Little Sisters of Jesus, spiritual heirs of Father de Foucauld, have exerted a great influence; other laymen are inspired by the religious orders, and many are involved in the family movement. It would be wrong to compare these evangelical fraternities of laymen with those groups which seek "perfection" and practice contempt for the world, groups which have always multiplied when the Church foundered. The fact that innumerable Christians ask to be educated, nourished, and helped by small communities does not prevent them from exercising their responsibilities in the world. This is how the Prior of the Little Brothers of Jesus has described their vocation:

The way of life of the Little Brothers of Jesus will always surprise people, since it does not fit the usual classification of the different forms of religious life. If you want to consider them as contemplative, you will be disappointed not to find in their fraternities all the conditions generally required for contemplative prayer—separation from the world, silence, and numerous regular hours of prayer. If, on the contrary, you want to consider the Little Brothers as religious who devote themselves to an active apostolate, you will be disappointed by their lack of strict organization, their refusal to take charge of a mission, a parish, or an organized activity—in a word, you will be impressed by an apparent inefficiency in their missionary activities.

Doesn't such a life risk disappointing those souls looking for a solid basis for monastic life aiming at union with God, and those eager for a missionary action which would be both efficient and in proportion to the needs of the apostolate in the modern world?

But the life of the fraternities will not disappoint those who are called to it by God, provided they are dominated by the unique desire to belong to Jesus, and to love him for

himself to the point of sharing with him the anguish of
man's salvation. The love of Christ for humanity became
the source of the apostolate at the time of his death on the
Cross. . . .

A Little Brother must run the risk of having an inadequate mode of action in order to remain close to Christ
loved for himself, as well as an inadequate mode of contemplation in order to remain an apostle to those who seem
most removed from Jesus. His apostolic activities are of
such a nature that they cannot be justified except in terms
of the imitation of Jesus, contemplated in his mystery of
weakness, agony, and death. . . . Without such constant
contemplation, a Brother would be tempted to fill his life
with more immediately efficacious activities, offering him
another center of interest. . . .

On the other hand, if a Brother should no longer feel an
anguished concern to work for the evangelization of man,
he could no longer support the most rigorous demands of
poverty and humble work, the price of his presence among
the forsaken men to whom he is sent.

The ideal of life of the Little Brothers, because of this
double demand of contemplation and presence among
men, and the means adopted for its realization, constitutes
an original form of religious life. The intuition which
brought Father Charles de Jésus* to inaugurate—without
knowing it—this new way of life, sharing the living conditions of the nomad Tuareg population. . . .

As for us, we shall not remain faithful to this ideal unless
we see everything in a unique love of Jesus. The light coming from the contemplation of the heart of Jesus, and from
our love for him, is the only thing capable of illuminating

* Religious name of Father Charles de Foucauld, who lived as a hermit
in the Sahara, at the beginning of the twentieth century.

the contradictory values of our vocation, and of making them a unity, with a simplicity which, in some matters, only a heart can confer.[6]

The Little Brothers of Jesus are not a model for all French Catholics; but, attracted by the examples of Charles de Foucauld and Thérèse de Lisieux, they represent a rather widespread tendency. Some French Catholics have even rediscovered the positive meaning of asceticism, and a few small communities dedicated to nonviolence have emphasized the practice of fasting. They have made clear that fasting is not a bizarre tactic of visionaries; in a number of their campaigns against hunger they have considered it a complement of almsgiving. As Father Régamey has said, fasting has become a crossroad where many old and new experiences in Christianity seem to meet:

The current situation in regard to fasting has a strange analogy with that which preceded Tertullian and the Council of Nicaea: general obligations have been almost eliminated, and individuals and communities are invited to show what they are capable of. There are only four fast days a year, and on those days "the new legislation authorizes such a variety of foods that, even when taken in small quantities, they do not make fast days very much different from others."[7]

As Father Bouyer has said, "The freedom the Church gives us now to determine for ourselves the forms and limits of our asceticism, far from meaning an irrevocable farewell to asceticism, is a providential opportunity to escape finally the confusion between spirituality and casuistry...."[8]

Three-fourths of mankind today is hungry: our communion with them urges us to support our prayers and efforts in their behalf by fasting. In our very flesh, we initiate a trend toward self-denial, of which the world is in special need at this time. . . . Now that competent, really efficient people are volunteering for peace tasks, the contemplative virtues—even among those who are most active —are again calling for discreet and silent fasting. . . .[9]

There are other related developments which should be mentioned. The annual pilgrimage students have been making to Chartres since the war, following Péguy's footsteps, attracts more and more people. The biblical movement is bearing its fruit—the Jerusalem translation of the Bible has achieved an extraordinary success. The four-volume *Initiation Théologique*, edited by a group of Dominicans, was read by many laymen. Reviews such as *Christus*, published by the Jesuits, have provided sound spiritual instruction. Because French Catholics have gradually acquired a more thorough biblical education, and because of the demands of our times, there has been a greater concern with personal prayer, understood as something more demanding than experienced, more desired than achieved.

Another sign of the times was to see Father G. Morel, a Jesuit philosopher and theologian, rereading St. John of the Cross in the light of modern philosophy, and reminding us that today, more than ever, mystical and historical experiences are compatible:

It is evident that the mystical expression of St. John of the Cross presupposes not only natural gifts but also an education and other advantages which most men do not have. But since mystical life is not definable simply by its conditions, it would be a Gnostic view to make it an essentially cultural phenomenon reserved to a certain intellectual or social aristocracy: every human being, no matter how anonymous, bears in his heart, even if he does not know it, the heart of a God which he can hear throbbing from the depth of distress. Love does not single out anybody; it does not belong to anyone by priority. It is not tomorrow, in the future, reserved to other generations, that men can begin to live and love, but here and now: the Sovereign Presence did not wait for our effort before offering himself, untiringly, in the obscurity of man's soul.

Only those who consider mysticism simply one form of human existence among others will take this as an alibi for laziness or cowardice in the task of transforming the universe. As St. John of the Cross has reminded us, love (mystical life) is not a substitute for nothingness. This does not mean the annihilation of structures and differences. Being infinite, God cannot present himself directly; this justifies nature and history, and therefore the phenomenal world. The historical becoming of humanity within nature will not restrict the place of love, but will extend its presence as much as possible in all the particular conditions of life. . . .

The limitations of St. John's teaching can be explained partially by the perspective of his time. We have a keener awareness today of inevitable determinations within empirical history, from the economic understructure to the ideological superstructure. We see clearly that the metamorphosis of these determinations is a necessary condition for the expression of each individual's genuine freedom (that is to say, love) and for its realization according to its own originality in the phenomenon.

Such a transformation requires effective recognition of the divine presence in the human flesh. The passage from darkness to light, if it is not simply an automatic process, cannot be reduced to economic or political liberation; it means the genuine creation of humanity. We have to begin again, in different conditions, and each in his own way, the enterprise announced periodically by the great mystics: to descend together toward the heart of beings and things, and after crossing the threshold of death, reappear in the true light. For those who do not think of themselves exclusively, this day is already dawning, however dimly: "Lord God, you are not distant from one who does not make himself distant from you. How can anyone say that you are ever away?" (St. John of the Cross)[10]

All these efforts, then, have led only to a further search. But in periods of change, fidelity requires a pilgrimage. One must not stop on the way.

We must wait and hope. It is too early for the experience of laymen to bear its fruits, for the world is searching for itself while the Church is searching for the world. To whom can we speak? What can we say that would be helpful? . . .

If we reject secular humanism, Simone Weil wrote, "Far from elevating ourselves, we abandon the last confused image we had of the supernatural vocation of man." But how blurred that image is! Abundance and power have manufactured a man who eats, travels, knows everything and no longer knows anything, a consumer who is in such a hurry he no longer has any present. He is being persuaded that thought, which chooses and declares something, is superfluous. Ideologies are dead, so they say. We have reached the paradise of objectivity where whores are sociologists. We shall soon be able to administer a world without mystery. The fashionable novelist hides behind objects —the fact is, the more he thinks he remains in the background, the more his nose shows. This must be what is called the dialectical progress of history. When we cease to consider our least ideas as plain reality we mistake things for gods. Let us wait for the next stage. It is too early to invent a humanism, and the worst blunder would be to manufacture a Christian humanism before its time.

Small prophets multiply. They look at the world from a distance, and pretend they are the Fathers of the desert. Yet it has never been so necessary to testify in favor of the few essential truths with which a Christian does not compromise. We should remember that no one seems more like a prophet than a fugitive. We need to learn the discrimination of spirits. It is not by accident that men like Paul Ricoeur and Father Régamey insist that we must bear the sin of violence like a cross in order to conquer it, and we must avoid isolation.

What then? Respect both the world and the faith; wait patiently for the time when we shall be able to decipher the meaning of this world; prepare a new civilization; and attempt to make manifest the demands of the Gospel. . . .[11]

V

The Secular City

The School Question

Historical developments have brought about a closer and more intensive interpenetration of Catholicism and politics in France than in any other country. The execution of the King at the time of the French Revolution achieved a break not only with a regime, but also with a social order in which the monarchy and the Church vouched for and upheld each other. The aftermath was civil war which, secretly or openly, has never ceased to divide France into two enemy camps: on the one hand, republicans, revolutionaries, and progressives, who were generally atheistic and anticlerical; on the other, conservatives—advocates of law and order who were either Catholics or were in alliance with the Church. This tangled strife of religion and politics endured throughout the whole of the nineteenth century.

The resulting confusion was such that any Catholic who went over to the Left was suspected of having repudiated his faith.

The situation had one advantage, however: the majority of Catholics, having openly declared against the Republic, grew accustomed to distinguishing between the authority of the Church and that of a state to which they attributed merely de facto power. This distinction was reflected at the beginning of this century when Church and State were officially separated; from then on, the Church, as it no longer received any grants from the state, could feel entirely independent of it. Faced with the modern reality of the secular state, Catholics tended to withdraw into their own circle; pitted against this atheistic and sometimes aggressively anticlerical state, they wanted to preserve at any cost their religious institutions, especially the one that hands down tradition and perpetuates the Catholic "species"—the school. Ever since the end of the nineteenth century, rival systems had been engaged in a fierce duel: Catholic ("free") schools vs. the public schools, which the Catholics called "godless."

Under the Third Republic Catholics as such played no part in the government. Most Catholic voters supported the conservative parties and, generally speaking, the reactionary coalitions; only a small minority took part in the Front populaire.* But the Second World War ushered in a new era. In the Resistance, the traditional party lines became blurred, and at the same time both the Christians and the Communists became more important. Until then, it had been difficult to consider Catholics as authentic republicans. However, it was a Catholic, one of the leaders of

* A coalition of leftist parties which came to power in 1936 under the Socialist Léon Blum.

Christian democracy, Georges Bidault, who became the head of the *Conseil national de la Résistance* (National Council of the Resistance) in 1943. From that time on, through the agency of this underground movement, a powerful trend to the Left gathered in French Catholicism. It was first represented by the *Mouvement républicain populaire*, the MRP, which at the beginning was a Left-center party; but there were also many Catholics in the largest and Communist-dominated union, the CGT, *Confédération générale du Travail;** some were even to be found in the ranks of the Communist party. It seemed, in 1944, that there was nothing to prevent Catholics from adopting a broad political pluralism, and co-operating with the Left. It soon became clear, however, that this hope was naïve, since the problem of the school remained unsolved.

As early as 1944, Henri Marrou, an authority on St. Augustine and a specialist in early Christian history, raised a storm of protest when he suggested the integration of denominational schools within the framework of a national school:

> It is a fact, regrettable perhaps, that for French Catholics of the generation to which the majority of our bishops belongs, the idea of religious freedom and even faith itself, is closely bound up with the school question. To put it plainly, this connection is empirical, it is sheer sociological relativism; on this point the historian can give guidance to theologians who, I feel, are often ill-informed. The denominational school is not a doctrinal requirement pertaining to the very essence of faith, but grew up out of a particular situation—the disappearance, during the barbarian days of

---

* A general confederation of labor unions, "apolitical" in principle but, in fact, divided several times since its foundation over the problem of its relations with the Communist party.

the early Middle Ages, of secular culture and schools; at that time the Church had to take on a task which secular society no longer fulfilled. But all through the patristic era, as long as the traditional schools of antiquity continued to exist, Christians were quite content with them while managing to conquer the whole pagan world. However, in order to avoid religious conflict . . . I suggest that wherever an objective analysis of the situation indicates that it would be desirable, a denominational school be maintained along with a "neutral" school. But this denominational school must be national, without tuition, and supported by the state; it must be integrated into the nation, serving it and not just a Christian ghetto. Like the "secular" school, it will be subject to the control, not only political, but also pedagogical, of the state. . . .

To my thinking, this denominational school is justified only in terms of the actual situation, which is a temporary one; it corresponds to no ideal. For a believer, the ideal does not consist in the defense of a loyal ghetto but in irradiating the people of France with Christian faith. I am ready to maintain before a council of bishops that the "priest school," which quickly becomes distasteful, is no remedy, but that faith will be saved in France by an apostolate exercised within a secular environment on the lines of the Young Christian Students' movement.

From a national point of view, however, unity is the ideal to strive for, a unity that, of course, does not exclude the legitimate diversity of spiritual families, but presupposes a common denominator. In fact, Christians coexist with unbelievers in France; public welfare urgently requires that they not only live side by side but as a community; accordingly, they must stop looking at each other as monsters. The ideal solution does not lie, as in Belgium, in the juxtaposition of schools serving rival ideologies but

*in the establishment of a single school in which children
from the most diverse backgrounds come together and
learn to respect, understand and love one another. Catholic
teachers would join such a school on their own responsibility, as many of them already have, to safeguard the legitimate rights of Catholic families. The first imperative which
should govern partisan minds, whether secular or Chris-
tain, is to restore the common desire of the French to
establish one nation; the school must serve this common
purpose.*[1]

Marrou was touching the most sensitive point of traditional Christendom. For the hierarchy, to give up the confessional school meant to give up the opportunity to train a
certain percentage of Catholics and to lose a main source
of priests. But to keep their own schools meant, for all
practical purposes, to choose traditional Christendom at
the cost of the modern world which the Church wished to
evangelize:

*Is it reasonable to have, in a town of 50,000 inhabit-
ants, twenty priests (as many as all the parish priests put
together) teaching regular sciences to the four hundred
pupils of the private secondary school when only one priest
attends to the two thousand pupils of the public schools,
eighty per cent of whom have made their first Communion?
Is not the first duty of the Church, before it teaches Latin
or mathematics, to impart the Word of God to those who
are baptized?*[2]

Marrou insisted that an authentic Christian faith would
break down the protective barriers erected by the Church.
The need of the national community was in agreement with
the call of the Gospel in this instance, the same call that
drove the missionaries to the factories:

It shocks me deeply, I admit, to see this timorous faith concerned exclusively with maintaining a small residual flock, recruited by birth and thinned by apostasy; a faith which, in meeting the unbeliever, sees only the possibility of loss. Does the baptized child who grows up within the Church never have anything to give?

That is why, from a strictly Christian point of view (not as a thesis, but in consideration of the position of Christianity in France today), we should strive for what I call a common, rather than a single, school system, where all the spiritual families of France would grow side by side in an atmosphere of mutual consideration, where the Christian child will feel as respected as any other, and with his faith strengthened through contact with beliefs other than his own, will be able to exert an influence—if he truly believes. . . .

If the word "ghetto" really seems too harsh, let us say that, since 1830, the Church of France has had an unfortunate tendency to emigrate inward, to see itself as an isolated whole, cut off from the rest of the nation. Captivity, deportation, and the Resistance have suddenly made many priests see the situation for what it is. Our bishops, and our clergy in general, live in splendid isolation; they never sit down to a discussion with anyone outside their own group. This is the crux of the matter: France is a divided country with regard to religion; a Christian must coexist with other Frenchmen who, unfortunately, are not Christians. National ideal and religious duty alike forbid him to claim the status of a privileged, indrawn minority. We must act accordingly; I do not see that we are prepared to do so.[3]

The Church and Civil Society

If we wish to understand it, the position of those Catholics who favored an integrated school should be seen in a broader context, taking into consideration all the relations between the Church and secular society. The time had come for the Church to give up a manner of presence that owed much to political power, and to seek other means of incarnation. This required that a certain distance be maintained between the temporal and the spiritual order. The action of God in history is usually indirect, leaving man the problem of understanding and the freedom of action. Emmanuel Mounier had formulated this Christian philosophy better than anyone else, including its application to commitment:

It is true that in France today the Christian world by and large is more shackled by a confusion of the orders than by too-fine distinctions between them. For several centuries, out of fear of the struggle between the angel and Jacob, of the naked dialogue of the Word of God and the music of this world, we have multiplied transitions, conciliations, amalgams until our faith today is bottled up to the stifling point. We feel the need of rediscovering pure essences and vigorous existences, Christianity in its supernatural clarity, the world in its detailed splendor, and their relationship in all its truth—obscure no doubt, but hard as diamond, not vague as mist. . . .

I am not forgetting that the conscience of the Catholic is not isolated in these difficulties. His life of faith is grafted onto the faith of the Church, not (if it is a living faith) in an exterior relationship of blind submission to authority but in a profound vital unity: sentiat cum Ecclesia. What then is the situation of the Church with regard to the reading of history? She, too, lives in the enigma of faith. The book with the seven seals will open only on the last day. The complete comprehension of history, and thus the full understanding of each of its moments, will be fully revealed only at that time—for the doctors and theologians as well as for the faithful. . . . Must we conclude that the teaching Church may be as unprovided as the natural reason for discovering the rationale of history in that partial, deficient, conjectural reading we are able to make of it? That would be to overlook the spiritual. This assistance does not imply that churchmen and theologians cast more light on the problems of civilization than do those who refer them to the natural reason, nor that they possess absolute evidence as to the ways of God, even in their supernatural destination. No one today, I dare say, would pretend to decide peremptorily whether the conversion of Constantine was a good or an evil for the Church, or whether a socialistic type of economic structure is better suited to the progress of the Kingdom of God than a capitalist economy. But the Church is assisted by the Spirit in its power of direction, and this direction, although bearing directly on sacred history, cannot, in the organic connection of the orders, fail to bear at least indirectly on profane history, on its intelligence, on the choices which must be made there.

The Church is herself assigned her limits in this reading of history and she has in doctrine kept within them more resolutely than the practice of her clerics would indicate. Against the Caesaro-Papist theses she has maintained that civil society and its powers, reason and its capacities, have a natural autonomy within their own orders. It has been possible to say that the idea of the laicity of the state and of society is a Christian idea and is guaranteed only by a vigorous concept of transcendence. Today the Church withdraws from many quarrels in which she has been a contending party since the Middle Ages. It is not so much that she renounces her presence in the world as that she concentrates rather on the most essential factor—indeed on the most pressing aspect of her presence—which is not external display, even less an imperialism, but an ardent discretion, even as the very presence of God.[4]

With a view to a thorough overhauling of the relations between the Church and civil society, two professors, Joseph Vialatoux and André Latreille (one from the secular, the other from the denominational school system), had drawn up, in 1949, a basic text which contained extremely clear definitions:

When the state and its national institutions are laic, this means simply that a citizen is not required to have a religious faith in order to live as a loyal citizen, without restriction and with full rights in the national and civic order. This means that the domains of Church and State are radically distinguished by the act of faith, that is to say, by the essentially free act which defines liberty itself. The state (and still more, any society of nations) expresses all of human life short of the act of faith, or rather of the act of liberty which decides it; the entire temporal order is its common estate. The Church expresses the life of the act of faith. Consequently, laicity juridically expresses the very liberty of the act of faith. It is solely the legal projection of the living consciousness of the liberty of the religious act. It is the guarantee of this very liberty. . . .

The principle of laicity was supported by Christianity when it declared itself essentially supernatural, coming from on high, above the efforts of humanity. Before the time of Christ such a clear distinction between state and religion was impossible. The state was religious, but this was not because it recognized a supernatural domain which it could not itself affect; on the contrary, reducing religious sentiment to the Eros, to the human effort toward divinity, the state was able to consider religion as part of its domain.

The Emperor was Pontifex Maximus. Christianity alone made possible the distinction between Church and State for it declared itself above the state, answering from on high a human desire in such an original manner that it permitted religion to develop for itself, and on the other hand, allowed the state to find its proper realm. It is striking to note how little positive aid in preaching the Gospel St. Paul expects from the state. . . .

True laicity, far from being the expression of a kind of totalitarianism, is rather an expression of reserve on the part of the state, the recognition of its natural limits. By it the state acknowledges that it is not qualified to bind the soul in the zone of its greatest liberty. It does not consider itself the necessary milieu for the ultimate finality of the spirit. An authentically laic state will be the least totalitarian of states, for totalitarianism on the part of the state consists in pretending to be the expression of all the spiritual powers of man. A lay state as such stops short of the freest and most decisive aspirations of man; it is forbidden by definition to be totalitarian. . . .

This ideal laicity can be called neutrality inasmuch as it denies itself the decision concerning the form which the act of religious liberty will take; it is neutrality of choice. But it is not the neutrality of someone who is unaware of religion or who scorns it. On the contrary, the lay state is conscious of being entirely at the service of the liberty of the human spirit; it considers the nation—of which it is the "authority" —as essentially the milieu where the development of the spirit and the exercise of liberty is made possible. It maintains then that the highest activity, to which it is servitor, is the conscious and free act, and its whole role consists in making possible the exercise of this conscience and liberty. But it cannot ignore the fact that the supremely free act is the one in which man responds to the problem of his destiny, and that from all time it is religion which has provided the societies where answers to this problem may be worked out, and that the answer to this problem is essentially of the religious order, the religious act itself. Whatever the answer to the religious problem may be, the lay state, if conscious of its laicity, would recognize that national life culminates in the religious problem, that the final end of religious societies is superior to its own, and that it can only provide possible members for them. It will not occur to this state to make its citizens members of one religion or another, but it will occur to it to procure for all men the conditions of development, of knowledge and of liberty so that all men might easily and clearly settle for themselves the religious problem. From this point of view, it is clear that the refusal of all religion is itself an act of religion, since this would be for man the choice of his destiny. For the lay state, "free thought" would be beyond the religious problem; it would already be an answer.

What the Church cannot admit is a state acting so as to render it difficult for a man to pose in all clarity and resolve in full freedom the religious problem for himself. If such a state existed, only men of genius could comprehend the importance of the religious problem, and it would require true heroism in order to resolve the problem according to what one maintained to be the truth.

It is clear then that the state in its laws must take account of religions, not only to safeguard the natural human order from them, especially human liberty which they might be tempted to oppress (clericalism), but also to give them the space and time and all the necessary conditions to accomplish their mission. It cannot ignore, moreover, the relative importance, for its nationals, of one religion or another, and must desire, in its necessary relations with religions, to give them all the same importance. On this

*point it has only to remain faithful to facts which can vary
under the influence of liberties. But the preference which it
accords to this or that religion is guided by this national
importance, not by the recognized "truth" of religion; it
depends on sociological facts, not on spiritual principles.*[5]

The wrangling over the school was to continue. At every
election it enabled the parties of the Right to bring pressure
to bear on the hierarchy: wouldn't a victory of the Left
mean the end of the Catholic school? The MRP, hamstrung
by this demagoguery, practically gave up proposing a reform of the school law.

The question whether the secular state could have any
rights as against the requirements of the Church was
brought to the attention of the public in the Finaly case, a
violent conflict whose issues roughly paralleled those of the
school debate. It was revealed in 1955 that two young Jewish boys had been kidnaped by Catholics. The parents of
the boys, before their own deportation, placed them in the
charge of a Catholic woman. This woman had the children
baptized after their father and mother died in concentration camps. However, after the Liberation, surviving members of the Finaly family tried to recover the children. The
Court ordered that they be returned to their family, but the
woman refused to obey and hid them in a convent, from
which they were taken to Spain. This unhappy affair
epitomized the whole problem of the relation of Church
and State. Were Catholics entitled to refuse to obey the law
in order to keep two ten-year-old children in the Church?
Among Catholics there were two conflicting opinions: that
the secular state could not possibly have any rights in such
a case; and that secularism represented, as Latreille and
Vialatoux expressed it, "the legal guarantee of the freedom
of the act of faith." Despite the strong opposition put up by

the integralists in this case, the Church of France bowed to
the independence of the state.*

The same thing also happened on other, less complicated, occasions. A recognition of the state as guarantor of
religious tolerance seemed to be an acquired fact. Cardinal
Gerlier, Archbishop of Lyons, solemnly affirmed it in a
speech (August 1958) in which he repudiated clericalism
and drew a distinction between secularity and secularism:

> The secular character of the state can be understood in
> very different ways. If the sovereign authority of the state
> over some field of the temporal order, its right to manage
> by itself the whole organization of society, political, judi-
> cial, administrative, fiscal and military is meant, this under-
> standing is fully consonant with the doctrine of the
> Church. . . .
> If the secularity of the state is understood in the sense
> that, in a country where there are many different persua-
> sions, the state must let each citizen freely practice his reli-
> gion, this second meaning, if correctly interpreted, is also
> in agreement with the teaching of the Church. The Church,
> of course, deplores the fact that there are many different
> beliefs. But it also insists that the act of faith be made
> freely. It therefore asks simply to be free to carry out the
> spiritual mission entrusted to it by its divine founder.
> But should the secularity of the state become—God
> forbid—a philosophy implying a materialistic and atheistic
> concept of human life and society, and turn into a system
> of political government under which this philosophy would
> be imposed on the civil servants, the public schools, and the
> whole nation, then we would have to denounce it with all

---

* The Finaly children were brought back from Spain and returned to
their family, who took them to Israel, after having promised to let them
choose their religion when they came of age.

our *strength and condemn it in the name of the true mission both of the state and of the Church.*

Having just witnessed a costly war which was fought to liberate people from totalitarian doctrines, could we possibly advocate a concept of secularity which would do violence to the conscience of France's citizens and shatter all hopes of national unity?

Finally, let me add that, should secularity come to mean a deliberate refusal on the part of the state to bow to any higher moral order, and an intent to found its action on self-interest alone, we would have to say that this is a dangerous thesis, retrograde and false.

Dangerous because it takes us back to the concepts of the pagan state from which Christianity freed us, while progress achieved by modern law has tended toward a limitation of the absolute power of the state.

False because nothing can prevail over ethics and law, and because ordinary legality does not itself constitute law.

Pluralism in Politics

However, if the Church of France had now recognized secularity for the state, secularity was soon to create difficulties once again in the political field. Neither the pluralist tradition mentioned above nor the experience of the Resistance were sufficient to guarantee Catholics complete freedom in their commitments. It was not only the school question which drove Catholics back to the Right; it was also, increasingly, anticommunism. The Cold War has gone on since 1947; the Soviet Union was intensifying its hold over the people's democracies; the Church was undergoing persecutions in the Ukraine, Yugoslavia, Czechoslovakia, and Poland. Western Europe felt threatened. In Italy, the link between the Vatican and the Christian Democrats had become closer and the "political unity" of Catholics began to sound like a new dogma. These developments soon exercised their influence over France, particularly within the MRP.

In 1945 this party had seemed like a real innovation in French politics; open to the Left, it enjoyed the support of the hierarchy, which felt the need to be forgiven for its favorable attitude towards Marshal Pétain; at that time it won twenty-seven per cent of the vote. But in 1947, its Right wing swamped by the Gaullists, the MRP lost two-thirds of its support. From then on, it tried to win back votes by abandoning its leftist positions, by championing the cause of the Catholic school and helping to repress the independence movements which were breaking out in the French colonies. Little by little, it became a Right-Center party, forsaken by those who were shocked by the brutal handling of the strikers in France and the natives in Madagascar and Morocco.

As early as 1948, Joseph Hours, one of the forerunners of the MRP, detected some of the reasons for its failure:

The men of the MRP imagined that generous yearnings of a philosophical or religious nature were enough to constitute political thinking. They thought that with this meager equipment, they were prepared to grapple with the perils of government under exceptionally difficult circumstances. Lacking any comprehensive grasp of the major constitutional, economic, military or colonial problems, they tackled each one separately; is it any wonder that they were overwhelmed?[6]

The gradual return of the Catholic masses to the Right especially benefited the Conservative and Gaullist parties, because the MRP did not agree with one of the favorite positions of the Right. The MRP had declared itself for European unity and had campaigned under its distinguished leader, Robert Schuman, for the establishment of a "European army" as an indispensable preliminary to the institution of a supranational authority. The European question had brought a great deal of confusion into the ranks of the French Left. A large part, including the Communists, was resolutely hostile, looking at the "Europe" that was envisaged as the work of capitalists supported by the Vatican. Much of the Christian Left agreed with them. Aside from political considerations, they had special reasons for this feeling: they were afraid that this European unity might spell victory for the "political unity" of Catholics within the Christian Democratic parties, which already had the upper hand in Italy and in Germany. In addition, a certain amount of Gallicanism seemed to have come to life again as a result of the increasingly stern measures taken by the Vatican against "French innovations." In 1953, the Papal Nuncio, Cardinal Roncalli, himself intervened directly in the priest-worker affair.

The year 1954 brought new dimensions to the problem of the politcial commitment of Catholics: The war in Indochina, for which the responsibilities of the MRP were considerable, had ended in defeat; and the Left came into power for the first time in six years, under Pierre Mendès-France. The MRP headed the opposition, suspecting him of designs upon Europe and of hostility to the confessional schools; furthermore, Mendès-France was a Jew, and this aroused the more or less secret antagonism of Catholic reactionaries. Controversy was raging among French Catholics; the MRP and the Catholic Right fought Mendès-France in the name of Europe and in behalf of a Christian civilization that they identified with the French Colonial

Empire; other Catholics denounced the coalition of Catholicism and colonialism and stated that they would rather
have a Premier who didn't go to Mass, provided he pursued
a policy of justice and of peace. The Mendès-France government fell, but Mendès-France ran as leader of the *Front
républicain* in the elections of January 1956. The Catholic
Left had received invaluable support from a man whose
talent for polemics seemed to have grown keener with age,
François Mauriac. It was at this point that Mauriac most
vehemently affirmed the political freedom of Catholics and
their right to vote for the Socialist and "Mendèsist" candi-
dates of the *Front républicain:*

*"We Catholics refuse to be the exclusive possession of
the reactionary groups in the Assembly any longer. We
reject this underhanded use of Catholicism which has now
lasted for five years . . ." That is the theme of the letters I
receive every day from Christians who cannot reconcile
themselves to sacrificing their immense hope of resurrection to a law on school grants.*

*The time has come to expose this ambiguity and to speak
loud and clear. We are not afraid of the word secular. We
dread it far less than its antonym—clerical—and not in
spite of our faith, but because we are Christians.*

*We, the laity, are not afraid of this word, but neither are
our bishops.*

*I suggest to those of our correspondents—there are some
—who are giving up the fight for fear of aiding and abet-
ting the opponents of the Church, that they study the
prophetic lines written by Bishop Mignon, of Chartres, and
quoted by one of our colleagues in a morning paper; they
express what I have always thought secretly (but we laymen are a little shy on these subjects . . .) "The new*

Christianity will no longer be sacral and clerical but profane and secular. This means that institutions will no longer devote themselves directly to the development of the Christian faith and of religious values but to the promotion of genuine human values. Ambiguous values, undoubtedly, are as apt to work for good as for evil. It is for Christian laymen to endow with meaning, scope and a hope of fulfillment all those things that would otherwise remain neutral or become bad."

Of course, Christians are free to look either to the Right or the Left for a solution. But they are not free where charity is concerned. They are not free with respect to justice.

The Bishop of Chartres is here reminding us of this truth. Christians, while they must render to Caesar the things that are Caesar's, may never violate the enduring principle of charity "which," he adds, "can be of great significance—we are too often inclined to forget it—as regards the choices we make in the temporal field, because their nature is so intimately connected with a specific concept of man and of justice." There is no better way of expressing it: a choice in secular matters impels us, as Catholics, to support the Left, not in spite of, but because of, our faith.

It was through no fault of ours that a human—that is, Christian—policy was not put to us by Christian politicians. We are not responsible for the fact that certain Catholics have ratified disasters resulting from a short-sighted Machiavellianism which they would have shunned had they but reflected on a single word of their daily Our Father.

The important point is not that our ministers go to Mass every day, but that they restore the state and serve justice, whatever the order to which it pertains.

Officially, the Church is not participating in the debate. We were warned in a communiqué recently issued by the Secretariat of the French Hierarchy: "In order to affirm the independence of the Church and keep it out of the political arena, the assembled cardinals and bishops of France remind the public that no candidate to election may stand as a Catholic candidate or allege membership in a Catholic organization in support of his candidacy."

The Church is not clerical. In politics, very often, it does not use laymen so much as laymen use it. I am told that, at this moment, Premier Pinay's emissaries are trying to persuade our bishops to issue directives advocating a vote for the Right. It would seem that Cardinal Feltin, more than any other, is being overwhelmed with requests of this kind.

For our part, to those young Catholics who ask us, we say: even by the light of Christian conscience, you have no right to make your vote, which concerns the future of France and the peace of the world, depend on the fight over Catholic schools. . . .

If there is one man who cannot be suspected of any intent to betray the concept of secularity, that man is Mendès-France. But he will not be diverted from the real problem, from the one question: to give back to our people self-confidence and faith in its future.

Young Catholics, do not squirm at the sight of a label. It is true that for once we have poured new wine into the wineskins of the old parties. But do not be afraid of a word. Seek the Kingdom of God and justice; where justice lies, there lies the Kingdom of God.[7]

This sensational article drew a retort from the *Osservatore Romano*. Far from surrendering, Mauriac objected to the nonofficial "intervention" of the Vatican in French politics; and in an article which he published two days before

Christmas, he also expressed his indignation at this habit of Right-wing Catholics of denouncing their political opponents to Rome and of trying in this manner to implicate the Vatican in French political conflicts:

INTERFERENCE

"In no case," decides the Osservatore Romano, "may Catholics vote for an avowed enemy of their faith whose action tends, directly or otherwise, toward the destruction of the Church or even of every religion." I wish I could rest assured that no confusion has arisen in the mind of our Roman colleague between these two epithets: foreign and hostile. What is foreign to Christianity may well not be hostile to it. What is hostile to it may well not be foreign.

While he was in power, did Pierre Mendès-France utter one word, do any one thing that disturbed the conscience of Catholics? We remember his visit to the Vatican, the welcome that the Holy Father extended to him. Mendès-France rejected war; wherever he could, he stopped bloodshed.

On the other hand, yes or no, has the policy of all those people who are forever quoting the Church, who openly solicit the votes of Christians, has it not, grievously—and in full view of the whole world—offended Christian conscience? They are the ones who could indeed be called enemies! . . .

The Right has served the shady side of French policies over the last ten years. That is to say, what is known today as the Right: a polite expression referring not to a doctrine, but to wealth. Do not hope that the Christians whose letters appeared in this paper yesterday will ever give in to foreign pressure, even if it is applied by the Osservatore Romano; least of all if it comes from that quarter, for their primary concern is precisely to break the political bonds which are forever being formed anew between the Church and the powers for which Christ refused to pray when he said, "I do not pray for the world."

That is what these Christians are fighting for, and the spiritual failure of the MRP has now doubled the urgency, the intensity of the battle. . . .

The little child expected during the night of Saturday to Sunday will be born in prison, jealously guarded by a caste and by a class. All we can do is try to free him.[8]

Avant-garde Christians in France had steadfastly rejected the idea of a "Catholic Party." Abbé Boulier, who later joined the Movement for Peace, gave a categorical "No" to the Christian Democratic movement in 1946:

Christians are not expected to bear witness in France by managing the state and becoming identified with it; their ideal is different and it would be impossible to bring all the Christians in France into one party.

The falling away of the masses notwithstanding, the Christian religion still exists in France, but diffused, so that, in spite of the mistakes and follies of our nation, in spite of, or perhaps because of, its apparent secularism, its policy has remained that of a "most Christian" country. There is a continuity between the France of St. Louis and that of Léon Blum. Seen from abroad, it is obvious. We are all Christians in France and react as Christians, even, or especially, the so-called secularists.

But when certain Christians decide to bear witness, what they really intend . . . is to draw attention to, and then attract sympathy for, their special brand of Christianity.

Now, there is nothing astonishing in the fact that Christians are to be found in every political party. As Christians have all kinds of interests and therefore judge matters from very different points of view, they necessarily consider the action of the state from different angles, and are thus led to adhere to opposing groups.

What is it, then, that will bring Christians from different political parties to unite as Christians for one common political action?

It is not, it cannot be, the concerns or the program of a party. It is a more general "cause," transcending all parties, which will dominate their members and summon them to labor for a higher and more pressing need.

Some will contend that patriotism and religion constitute the "cause"; that Christians must strive actively, outside of parties and partisan politics, to bring about a sound nationalism and to protect religion.

We cannot prevent Christians from holding such opinions or from devoting themselves to the patriotic and religious action that such ideas call for, because we respect their freedom, which guarantees our own. We merely say that they are misguided Christians. The idea of Christianity lost ground in France in part through nationalist agitation; Christians professing to defend the country, the army, and the Church as one cause at the time of the Dreyfus affair brought upon the Church all the humiliation which is the usual fate of a defeated party. . . .

Should Christians institute a "Christian" party, no very definite program would differentiate it from others. Opposed to other parties, and thwarted by them in the melée of conflicting interests and the fierce scramble for posts and patronage, it would soon be reduced to some vague league of do-gooders, unless it settled into a small clan of sectarians. . . .[9]

A year later, Emmanuel Mounier denounced the developments that were leading Christian Democracy to the adoption of a "middle-of-the-road" policy.

By a strange quirk of fate, the Christian Democratic parties, founded in order to break the bonds that tied the Christian world to reactionary forces, are now in danger of becoming their ultimate refuge. Originally meant to oppose the alliance between the throne (or the bank) and the altar, they now tend, fifty years behind history, to substitute for the Holy Roman Empire and the Christian Monarchy a kind of "Holy Democracy," endowed with the same ambiguous characteristics. The bold ideas of our grandfathers are not going to allay the anxieties of our children. Middle-of-the-road clericalism is not going to uproot conservative clericalism. Not so long ago, to be a Christian meant, in the eyes of many, to be a reactionary. For men today, who must live with the terror of the atomic bomb, is being a Christian going to seem something like being a Radical-Socialist? If Christianity err, let it do so in style at least, boldly, defiantly, unafraid of risks and with passion. . . . [10]

The concern to avoid fusing politics and religion through a "Christian ideology" prompted Father Montuclard to set the respective limits of faith and politics:

The most basic kind of realism suggests that the essential component of Christianity is not Christendom but the Church; not Christian humanism but faith. It is impossible to reduce the Church to the juridical dimensions of a pure society. . . . Belonging to the Church is not, fundamentally, a reasoned acceptance of the articles of a creed but a different manner of living predicated on belief in the coming of the gift of God. To enter the Church, therefore, is not to choose between Christian doctrine and some kind of a philosophical system. It is not an option but the free ratification of the real predicament of man, caught, whether he likes it or not, in the interplay of love and of grace. . . .

Political action is merely the deliberate extension of the
meaning of the day's work to a more general, but still connected, area. The same interests are involved, the same
values sustained, whether false or true. Politics is not an
unselfish devotion to a pure ideal; it means using the soli-
darities and the oppositions which cause the struggle for
life until power has been seized and organized.[11]

Camus had accused Christians of not wishing to enter
the conflicts of this world on equal terms with unbelievers.
But, more and more, believers seemed to agree with
Domenach's insistence that in politics the cause of Catholics should not be dissociated from the common cause:

Some will say: we must safeguard the interests of the
Church, its institutions, the organic basis of its existence
and the means to ensure the possibility of its apostolate.
Yes, we must safeguard them, and no Catholic may drop
this major concern from his political program. But the way
to safeguard them does not consist in turning them into an
object distinct from other objects, a freedom distinct from
other freedoms; if we do that, we shall be trapped again by
special attitudes which will cut us off both from Christian
and from political universality, and finally confine our faith
behind the barriers of a class, a regime, or an economic
system. Catholics must state what they want; is it real freedom, the kind that is valid for all men, or is it their own
particular brand, freedom for their worship, their schools,
their press? These liberties are essential to the faith, but
they are inseparable from basic freedoms. We made that
discovery under Nazi Occupation, as the Poles have under
the Soviets. It is impossible for Catholics to continue to
defend their religious freedom successfully if at the same
time they tolerate, and sometimes even participate in, the

crushing of other liberties by economic exploitation, colonial oppression, or military dictatorship. It is impossible to advocate freedom in Poland and stifle it in Spain. Catholics, in defending the rights of their Church, should recognize that, in political strife, they are on equal terms with everyone else, and that the temporal good they fight for is not their exclusive privilege but the common good. . . .

Circumstances are forcing us into this practical secularity. Political life ensures communication between men within a given nation, and it is nowadays compelling the nations themselves to collaborate for world unity. Stripped of the political passions which covered it over, secularity appears to be, first of all, an intrinsic part of the very nature of the state; it is to politics what systematic atheism is to science—not a doctrine but a premise of research, a discipline of knowledge, and a requirement of action.

Secularity is more. It is also the barrier which we, believers or not, erect together to prevent any subjugation of the state by totalitarian philosophies. In their thinking about the state, Catholics should endeavor to rid themselves of memories of nineteenth-century conflicts. The secular state has been tempted, like all states, by abuses of power, and has succumbed, but less often than confessional or partisan states. Eric Weil says rightly that as a technique the state is neutral, but it becomes totalitarian when it yields to an idea. . . . Secularity is, therefore, the best guarantee of protecting political conscience from hypertrophy and society from idols.

This guarantee also applies to the Church insofar as it is tempted to build up, directly or indirectly, the apparatus of a state—police, propaganda, parliamentary techniques—which would lower it to the status of one political institution among many. Joseph Vialatoux and André Latreille have shown how this type of secularity is not an equal indifference to all beliefs but a personal and ecclesiastical affirmation of faith. . . .

The aim of political life should be, as Eric Weil expressed it, "that no one is forced to choose between God and Caesar," meaning that no one who has opted for God should be martyred by an idolatrous Caesar, just as no one should be enslaved by a Caesar who calls himself Christian. For a believer, the ultimate objective of politics is to enable as many human beings as possible freely to choose and to love God.[12]

Christianity and Socialism

But this did not mean that politics should be separate from religion. There was a link between the two. If the Gospel did not prescribe any specific policy, it was nevertheless from the Gospel that the socialist Christian would draw inspiration for his socialism:

We are not trying, as some "Christian socialists" have done, to trace socialism back to the Gospel. Broad economic planning and socialization of the means of production are technically debatable measures which include certain dangers to human freedom and dignity. Nevertheless, although he does not conceive of it as a logical requirement of his faith, a Christian manifestly derives his socialism from Christian sources. We are socialists because we consider that capitalism is incapable of solving the problem of underdeveloped countries, a momentous problem indeed for a Christian conscience; because we think that a greater equality in economic and social conditions will bring men together and prevent new wars. . . . We are socialists because we are personalists, not because we are Christians. But those of us who are Christians find in their religious faith compelling reasons to believe in persons. As Jeanne Hersch wrote, "Socialism does not include a religious 'creed,' which is why it does not conflict with religion. It does require, however, that its adherents turn to a religious or philosophical absolute, in order to substantiate the unde-fined value underlying the human person."*

But socialism has been condemned several times by the Holy See, some will say. It has, indeed—but with qualifica-tions and specifications.** ("Socialism," said Pius XI, "if it remains truly socialistic . . .")—for the Papacy was aiming at those concepts which socialism owed in part to its founders and in part to the dialectics of contemporary con-flicts: atheism, secularism, state control. Socialism is not yet entirely free from these concepts, but Stalinism has has-tened its evolution: the socialist insurgents of Budapest and the socialists of the workers' committees in Poland demanded the liberation of the worker from the tyranny of a materialistic system. Whether or not they were believers, they tied socialist claims to the perennial struggle of the human person. The connection between socialism and philosophical materialism is being severed, not only by the reflection of humanist theoreticians, but also through the workers' concrete fight against tyranny and by the blood they shed. A new road has been opened up. The statist absolutism inherent in certain socialist doctrines and pro-phetically denounced by the Vatican is challenged today within "socialist" countries themselves. The whole theoreti-cal and institutional system of materialistic socialism will have to change in order to find new foundations, not in

* Hersch, Jeanne, *Idéologies et réalitiés; essai d'orientation politique* (Paris: Plon, 1956).
** Cf. "Le socialisme et la doctrine de l'Eglise," by R. Heckel in *Revue de l'Action Populaire*, April 1957; and Herve Chaigne, "The Church and Socialism," in *Cross Currents*, Spring 1965.

religion, but in personalistic concepts acceptable to Christians.

"The majority of non-Communist socialists," writes Father Heckel, "put great emphasis on the dignity of man and clearly see that the gigantic productive and political organism cannot develop harmoniously unless trained citizens control it and are responsible for it. But do they think of also giving man that 'spiritual supplement' which would make him equal to his task?" Are believers, then, going to insist that unbelievers make a spiritual contribution—which, by definition, they do not possess? This is a strange requirement, indeed, and one which would preclude collaboration in the affairs of the secular city! Institutions and political principles can be shared by all; it is up to Christians to infuse them with their own spirit, to put their soul into them, or a part of their soul, for religious conscience can never be swallowed up by politics unless it has taken on the unwholesome aspects which we have denounced above. Conscience in politics means to care for others, in a practical, concrete* way; that is the greatness of politics in an age when it is becoming universal and when some of its decisions constitute a collective intervention of charity.

Does this mean that politics today can take the place of charity? Definitely not: Christianity means, first, the love of God, of one's self and of others for the sake of God. In the political field, conscience remains mediate, permeated with violence and error, directed to groups and not to the individual person. But it is here that a Christian recaptures this sense of belonging to one single people, this awareness of the human substance which had been lost through centuries of individualism; here that he can put love—so often pro-

* There does exist, as Paul Ricoeur brought out, a Christian praxis. A Christian is known by his deeds. Cf. *Les chrétiens et la politique*, by Henri Guillemin and others (Paris: Editions du Temps présent, 1946–1948).

claimed and so seldom practiced—to the test. Charity does
not spend its whole substance in politics, but at least it can
show its value there.[13]

What, then, were the imperatives of charity? Henri
Bartoli, an economist, advocated the unrestricted commitment of Catholics on the side of the workers:

We have tolerated the existence of inhuman social conditions, we have sometimes covered up their disgrace with the
name of God, and we cry shame because the Church has
lost the working classes. How can a man struggle to save
his soul when his whole life tends to deprive him of the
knowledge that he has a soul to save? How can the victims
of our affluent society feel anything but deep resentment
for the Christian world and Christian doctrine when they
discover all too often that the Church and the rich are in
collusion?
Legislation cannot effect a transfer of power from capital to labor in our society. Many existing laws are not en-
forced. In spite of the laws enacted in 1945 and 1946,
there are many enterprises with more than fifty employees
which have no workers' committees. In many concerns the
workers have no representatives. In too many factories,
overtime is paid at the regular rate, the higher rate provided by law is not applied, and offenders cannot be punished.
The freedom of trade-unionism has been proclaimed, it
is true, but the actual conditions of hiring, promotion, and
firing constitute pressure against activists, who are often
persecuted in the name of anticommunism.
If the ratio of salaries to national income is now about
the same as in 1938, it is not due to social security but to
longer working hours. Because their hourly wage is so low,

furnace workers put in seventy-two hours every other
week, and maintenance shifts work thirteen days on end,
with one Sunday off every fourteen days. Thirty-seven vat
workers out of forty in Toulouse resort to clandestine work
in order to balance their budgets. As for North African
workers, they are usually paid far less than the regular
wage and their housing is an insult to God and humanity.
The minimum wage is calculated so rigorously that it includes, for instance, the purchase of one warm overcoat or
its equivalent every six years, and lodgings devoid of individual water outlets.*

Do not say that a "strong" government could correct
abuses. No arbitration is possible between capital and
labor. Even when political and economic power are more
closely bound together than ever before, we cannot expect
from the state decisions that take into consideration the
interests of both capital and labor. . . .

As Economie et Humanisme** declared: "Short of turning renegade, capitalism cannot become philanthropic. . . .
No matter how advanced the stage it is in, a study of capitalism will show it doomed to failure or inhumanity. We
are in a terrible dilemma which leaves us no choice but to
create a new system in a society as yet unknown." . . .
Our task is to fight for the age of labor, since history and
faith demand it. We should constantly remember that history is made by free men acting in concert, and freedom
must refashion its structures as well as its conditions. We
are not being asked to give in to events, but to bear
witness. . . .

---

* Cf. "La mise en application de la loi du février 1950," in *Revue
française du travail*, September-October, 1950.

** *Cahiers d'economie humaine*, No. 4, 1951, pp. 40 ff. *Economie et
Humanisme* is an economic research group founded by Father L. J. Lebret,
O.P., which has done pioneering work in many poor countries.

I am convinced that the science of economics should be ruthlessly scrutinized, exposing its lies and its alienations, and then built up anew, with labor as its starting point and its primary values the liberation of workers and of work itself. . . .

The primary requisite for the establishment of a society truly founded on the recognition of labor is that this society grow out of the workers' own action—that is, from the action of labor, farmers, and intellectuals.

The numerous attempts at interpreting the historical phenomenon of the intellectuals have clearly shown that throughout history their part has been to give homogeneity, conscience, and the means of expression to the various social groups which make this history. It is a fact: sociologists are inclined to admit that if social classes cannot be defined precisely, it is above all because they can be known and understood only in their movement. Capitalism builds in the midst of society the permanent basis for what Leo XIII called a "dangerous conflict." To refuse to see this conflict in terms of history would be side-stepping the issue. We must, on the contrary, discover the categories defining the genesis of the antagonistic classes, and the internal and profoundly human law that governs it.

The emergence of the classes at odds within the capitalistic system has been perverted on an enormous scale; yet these classes offer fruitful ground for the incarnation of brotherly love. Without any illusion that the proletariat has some kind of messianic role to play, we recognize that it is called to bear witness against the rule of money and for the emancipation of labor. The coming age of labor will have the features of the movements which are shaping it. Some of us have been asked to be present in these movements in order to serve them. All of us are asked to join in the future with them, even if our task is only to be their witness in our own environment.

Let no one object that, by underlining the temporal role of Christians, we are ignoring eschatology for the sake of historical time. Eschatology alone gives history a meaning by endowing it with an end, but what can an eschatology be that is not already present in time? . . .*

The primary sense of the Messiah's work is to "bring forth justice to the nations" (Isaiah 42:1). Messianic first means historical. Justice, freedom, and love are not Platonist ideas but initiatives taken by God in history through the events of salvation. It is not moral values that are eternal but their inexhaustible source—that is, God. . . .

Christianity must insert itself into the very organization of the economy, saturate its structures and its institutions. . . .

When we co-operate with the protests of workers who will not be treated like goods, or of the proletarians against the conditions which capitalism has meant for them, we are not being unfaithful but are choosing a religion of incarnation rather than of evasion.

When bread and wine become the sustenance of the community in the Eucharist, it is the Spirit that is given to us, beyond death and resurrection. Then it is that we receive our mission. We go back to our work, but it is done with the Spirit, and the temporal world becomes finer material for new sacrifices.

To experience the Mass is to experience eschatology. If we knew how to look at the Host, we would see in it the toil of our brothers. Without "the food which perishes" there would be no "food which endures to eternal life" (John 6:27). Can we let labor continue in bondage?[14]

Demands such as these went directly against what was usually known as "the social teaching of the Church."

* Jean Lacroix, Marxisme, existentialisme, personnalisme (Paris: Presses universitaires de France, 1950).

Bartoli stated his position more explicitly in another article
two years later:

Does anyone seriously believe that Christians who have
come to realize that a break with the system is necessary
could imagine that the social question will be solved once
employers and workers have recognized their "common
interests" and organized profit-sharing within an economic
system which would still be capitalistic (even if no longer
completely liberal)?

"The social doctrine of the Church," aside from the
ultimate ambiguity of the term,* seems to misinterpret the
economic and social context on which it should bear. It is
surprising and somewhat shocking, for instance, to find in
Directoire pastoral en matière sociale,** a publication approved by the French bishops in 1954, reservations expressed in regard to nationalizations made at a time when
both the economic progress and the moral soundness of the
nation clearly required their broadening. How many more
years will it take Catholics to realize the importance of
pressure groups and the extent to which the state is corrupted by private interests?...

What man, familiar with law, economics, or ethics, and
acquainted with the present techniques of capital accumulation, would dare to write that "the common good requires
that the private ownership of enterprises remain the general
rule"? Is it fair that the shareholders of joint-stock com-
panies should, through the plowing back of profits, ap-
propriate the fruits of everyone's labor? Do our bishops
believe that this crying injustice will be removed by profit-
sharing, when all the laws passed since 1917 to establish a

* See the introductory pages of L'Enseignement social de l'Eglise, by
Father Jean Villain (3 vols.; Paris: Spes, 1953–54).
** Published by Bonne Presse, Paris, 1954.

partnership between capital and labor have been a total failure? . . .* Who does not know that the very framework of modern capitalism, its holdings, its combines, absolutely requires a distinction between legal ownership and the actual power of control?

When we read on page 30 of the Directoire pastoral en matière sociale that "the fair profit of the capitalist, like the fair additional profit of the worker, must be subject to the risks run by the enterprise," we wonder what is meant. An economist knows how difficult it is to state precisely what is "normal" profit, but no one believes that in a modern economy profit accrues because of activity of an isolated concern. . . . Decline in the price of raw materials, changes of power or in the international situation, causing a sudden drop in the prices paid by the suppliers, and other related factors all affect the economic situation. . . .

Of course, I shall be told that the "fair profit" of the capitalist, like the "fair additional profit" of the worker, the "risks" that each must run, are being compared in the abstract, that they are "doctrinal entities" propounded by a theologian. That is precisely what an economist, especially if he is a Christian, cannot tolerate. Clerics are wont to draw a distinction between "the idea of the wage-earning classes" and the concrete and historical relationship which links the wage-earner and the capitalist, but the economy is a praxis and economic science, the science of the human relationships in production and in trade resulting from human labor and described in their historical development, is a normative discipline. We may suggest systematic explanations and norms which go beyond the data yielded by a strict analysis of concrete situations, but our categories

* Cf. Marcel David, La participation des travailleurs à la gestion des entreprises privées dans les principaux pays d'Europe Occidentale (Paris: Dalloz, 1954).

must at least keep some relevance to humanity, and our reasonings must lead back to reality with a view to changing it. . . . Our job is not to promote a "Christian economy," an idealistic systematization that events would quickly challenge, but to affirm our presence in the world and to pass on to it the Spirit we have received. . . .

St. Thomas contrasts the theological virtues, the object of which is God, with the moral virtues, which are directed to created ends and must be practiced for their own sake. From this to deduce the absolute autonomy of the temporal world would be to misrepresent the thinking of St. Thomas. As the fruit of human work, any economic and political system, unless it is radically immoral, is informed with a sense of justice. Justice being a "religious value"—if not, religion itself would be immoral—we must admit that the Church, as a hierarchical priesthood, has a right to speak in the temporal order.

Our faith, as an active response to God's intent, must awaken in our conscience a purposeful desire to transform the world. The plan to achieve this end is the believer's own, conceived of his own initiative and prompted by his own convictions. However, if conscience is always called upon to mediate, it does so differently—but always cohesively—depending on whether the matter pertains to the Church considered as the sign of God's purpose or to the world which is to be transformed according to divine thought. If we wish to avoid the pitfalls of both secularism and clericalism, we must recognize that the Church defines the thought of God but, as to economic and political plans, passes exclusively on the conformity or incompatibility of their intent with his purpose. Considered as a secular body, the Church's role is to undertake the transformation of the world by a creative action faithful to the will of God. The promotion of political, economic, and social plans is the province of the secular, not of the hierarchical, Church. . . .

We have reached one of those periods in history when, in the very name of the teaching of the Church, we should protest and face the actual conditions of faith as it is lived. In the Parable of the Sower, we have the seed that is the word of God and the soil that receives it and determines the pattern of its growth. Let us beware, for if we persist in teachings divorced from an evolving historical reality, and in advocating ambiguous solutions, we shall effect in many consciences a juxtaposition of what they believe and of what they agree to profess. The greater the tension, the greater the risk of dual consciences, of pitiless suffering, or, ultimately, of outright condemnation.[15]

However, this revolutionary commitment at the side of the working classes involved the problem that we had also encountered in the case of the priest-workers: militant labor was, for the greater part, Communist; the most important French labor union, the CGT, was dominated by the Communists. The Catholics who advocated leftist causes, therefore, often collaborated with the party. Were they to go one step further and take what they were offered, an alliance, if not outright integration? André Mandouze, one of the leaders of the Christian resistance movement, who had been the chief editor of *Témoignage chrétien,* unhesitatingly said "Yes." In 1948 he defined the positions which later became those of Christian progressistes:

We are now at an intermediary stage where, in spite of some progress, the spiritual and the temporal authorities are squabbling over the delimitations of their respective fields. . . . Obviously, Marxism encroaches on the spiritual order, and Christianity on the temporal; the encroachments

on both sides are probably interdependent. Be that as it
may, each camp would profit by refraining from overstep-
ping, however slightly, the other's boundaries. The recognition of limits is the basis of efficacy and even of truth. "To
possess the promise of eternal life" does not imply that one
holds the key to the problems of life on earth. . . .

The truth is that, in essence, the spiritual rightfully belongs to Christianity, just as the political field is rightfully
that of Marxism; and the Communist party is no more entitled to cavil at Christianity about the Last Things . . . than
the Church is entitled to question the right of Marxism to
choose its actual means to a temporal end. . . .

The risk of oversimplification notwithstanding, we say
that, with due regard for special vocations and excluding
any implication of Christianization of the Marxist masses
or of Marxization(!) of the Christian masses, Marxism—
even if it is utterly indifferent to the spiritual or objects to
it—must recognize the legitimacy of a spiritual field, just as
Christianity—even if it has no hold whatever on the political and considers it dangerous—must recognize the legitimacy of its existence. Christianity and Marxism will be
strong only insofar as each respects its own boundaries.
They will be influential to the extent that they admit of
other authorities in matters with which they are not competent to deal and should not deal. An organic combination of their respective endeavors might later be possible. . . .

The existence of progressisme is tantamount to an acknowledgment of another fact: no revolution is possible
without the Communists, but the Communists cannot
bring it about alone. The Marxists themselves have noted
this and have drawn for their guidance conclusions which
far outweigh mere tactical considerations.

The Christian progressiste is very openly and very definitely with the Communists in the fight they are currently

waging. . . . In the present circumstances and with the Communists now holding the position they have in French politics, there are only two ways of handling the question: to be with them or against them. I am with them for the reason stated above—namely, that although it is possible to be a progressiste without being bound by Marxist tenets, it is quite impossible to strive for a progressive policy while ignoring the Communists. . . .

In political life it is impossible to be simultaneously for capitalism and against it. To denounce the abuses of capitalism, as the Church does, leaves room for two distinct policies: either to endeavor to correct the abuses without challenging the validity of capitalism itself and thus really to defend capitalism; or else to put an end to the abuses by removing their cause. . . .

Our collaboration with the Communists in the political field results not from identical doctrinal views or systematic alignment, but from a practical consideration, namely, that in spite of all that we can hold against them, the Communists hold the most cogent political views backed by the greatest and soundest mass support, and have thus taken the lead in the political struggle, the field in which their efficiency is greatest.

Our collaboration with the Communists does not result from an inferiority complex but is simply an acknowledgment of their superiority in the field of politics. It protects us from the temptation that has beset Christians for centuries: to flee from the political battlefield when the time has come to charge. That is why our political discipline, which has in no way been imposed upon us—the Communist party is not entitled to give us orders—is nevertheless a real discipline. Its rules do not come down to us through hierarchical channels; our discipline is truly political.[16]

The *Union des Chrétiens progressistes* published its manifesto in November 1948. One year later, Cardinal Suhard cautioned the faithful against the positions advocated by the *progressistes* and specifically against "close and habitual collaboration with the Communist party." In addition, most leading thinkers of the Catholic avant-garde —for example, Emmanuel Mounier and Father A. J. Maydieu, editor of the important Dominican monthly, *La vie intellectuelle*—were expressing their own reservations. In March 1949 Maydieu wrote:

If, in France, a Christian is against any collusion between his faith and a political option, if he objects to drawing too-logical inferences between them, he does so all the more when it is a matter of collaborating with a political movement that is a danger to his faith, as Communism professes to be, and seems to have been for the last thirty years.

From a human point of view, the objectives of Communism are magnificent, and rightly appeal to a generosity fostered by a Christian civilization. Nevertheless, one should not rashly bring together two reagents as potent as Christianity and Communism, whose respective methods, aims, and requirements are so hard to reconcile. The likely result is a union somewhat like that of the praying mantis, or, better still, of spiders: one of the partners is emptied of its substance during mating and leaves its hollowed-out carcass to the stronger to adorn its web. And are "the children of light" sure that they will be more astute than the "children of this world," that they will not let themselves be drawn into lies, tricks, and systematic violence, all justified, it would seem, for the sake of discipline, efficiency, or flexibility? By adopting these methods, even if only for a time, are they not running the risk of impairing, little by little, the soundness of their Christian instincts? If they object to the methods, will they not be expelled as "heretics," or will they themselves not have to give up these dangerous allies?[17]

A decree was issued by the Holy Office in July 1949 prohibiting all regular collaboration with the Communist party. The leftist Christians accepted it, but protested against the political significance certain people attributed to it. The fact is that, because of the political situation in France from 1949 to 1956, Christian leftists were confronted with a tragic dilemma: they felt bound to fight the colonialist and anti-working-class policies practiced by the government, but this political struggle put them on the side of the Communist party, almost with it, whereas Rome had forbidden collaboration. An article by Paul Fraisse in *Esprit* suggests the problems they faced and their difficulty in finding a solution:

A Christian has no right to enlist God in his business deals and party elections; he must deal with temporal matters—whether politics, art, or science—in the light of his knowledge and of the findings of his reason. The decisions he must make, the course of action he must follow are not written down in heaven; he must create them within the human community, blessed in the knowledge, however, that any good that he does really comes from God. . . .

Mere words? Possibly, for the man who mulls over the problems but does not try, quite simply, to experience them. A Christian holds no monopoly on truth in the political field; he must fight for justice or truth together with those who apparently have the same objectives. This position causes no difficulties as long as the differences among Christians are unified by anticommunism.

In France, whether you support the royalty or the party

system, liberalism or technocracy, your orthodoxy is not suspect as long as you don't do anything that might help the Communists. And you must never share their point of view on any problem. But how can one possibly imagine that the objectives of the Communists are all intrinsically perverse? Every day there are Christians who have to acknowledge that on such and such a point, the Communists are right. . . .

The Church properly reminds us that Christians do not have the right to contribute to the success of Communist doctrine. But to work with, or along with, certain Communists in specific cases and toward specific ends does not mean working for the victory of Communist doctrine or even of the Communist parties. Where truth is served, where justice is upheld, surely no aid has been given to enemies of the Church of Christ. . . .

But if we give Communism the exclusive privilege of posing an authentic problem, we are also investing it with the exclusive right to find its own solution. We are then forced to resort to the police of the armed forces in order to halt Communism, but such a "crusade" is an acknowledgment of weakness, as well as crime. Let Christians remember the promise of Christ to be with them to the end of time, and let them move forward with men of good will, making a variety of political commitments without trying to enlist the Church on their side, and support their decisions without hurling papal encyclicals or episcopal statements at each other.[18]

The progressistes were in a delicate situation, not only in their relations with the hierarchy, but also with the Communist party, which was dissatisfied with a qualified cooperation subject to reservations and restatements. At the time, Stalinist intransigence was rampant and the Communists wanted none but dumb and totally obedient allies. Finally, in 1955, the Holy Office condemned *La Quinzaine*, the journal of the Christian *progressistes*. Its directors then demonstrated, by deferring to Rome, that they were not the heretics they were supposed to be, confident that the future would justify their efforts:

If the Church were merely a human institution protecting a certain political order or social doctrine, we would have every reason to break with it. If belonging to the Church means accepting Bonn's concept of Europe, defending private ownership of the means of production, or dreaming of collaboration between capital and labor, let it be said once and for all: many who are baptized would no longer remain in the Church.

But the Church was founded by Christ in order that his love might be known to all men. The salvation of Christ is wrought through the mediation of the Church. That is why attachment to the Church lies at the very roots of our being. Our readers realize that the confidence and the interest awakened by La Quinzaine found their meaning only within the framework of fidelity to the Church.

We have chosen to cease publication and we realize the gravity of our decision. We do not know how the Church will come to accept the values of a new civilization opposed to the old, of which Rome still seems to be a prisoner. But our faith in Christ compels us not to despair of his Church, and to remain certain that despite often discouraging appearances, the Church has the means by which to effect the changes required by the universal character of its message. . . .

We remain faithful to the Church and, equally, to our commitments to our fellow workers and our fellow combatants, whoever they may be. Any denial of the choices we have made, any breaking of the bonds of solidarity which we have formed, are out of the question. . . . Christians today have no right merely to watch the tremendous effort that is being undertaken for the welfare of humanity, the establishment of justice, and the spread of culture over wider areas. To strive with others for the achievement of these human objectives does not result from a weakened faith or some sinister influence of Marxism. On the contrary, it springs from the same impulse of faith which makes Christians leave their ghetto and set out to share the human effort. What is the distinctive mark of a Christian received at baptism, if it is not this rootedness in the Church of Christ, which links him with the salvation of the world and makes him concerned about all men? . . .

Friends of La Quinzaine, it is up to us all to hasten developments, to invent new approaches, to intensify the struggle for a world of justice and peace, and to give life and shape to the hope of Christ.[19]

The fate of the *progressistes* hurt many Catholics who were political activists. In 1956, however, the Hungarian Revolution and the ensuing Soviet repression robbed the Communist party of much of its prestige. Although it remained very important from the electoral point of view, it ceased to weigh so heavily on the conscience of the French Left. Certainly, the revelation of the crimes committed during the Stalinist era cost the party the halo it had had in the eyes of a certain number of young Christians.

After many mistakes and countless difficulties, at least the political freedom of Catholics had been achieved, as Jean Lacroix pointed out:

. . . I do not know exactly what it means to be a "rightist" or a "leftist"; still less do I understand the nature of a

Catholic "rightist" or "leftist." But I do know that more and more Catholics base their political options on reasons that have nothing to do with religion. It has now become impossible to impose a political position on them from the outside or through hierarchical channels. The Catholic who is a rightist—or leftist—because he is a Catholic belongs to a species that, fortunately, is dying out.

All the difficulties and all the problems, unfortunately, begin beyond this point. If a wish is in order, I would ask all Catholic movements to worry less about the political and civic education of the young and more about the formation of Christian consciences, equipped to make their own decisions in the political, economic and social fields, on their own responsibility, in the presence of God, within the communion of the faithful and for the good of all citizens, whether or not they are Catholics.[20]

The Development of Christian Trade-Unionism

Parties and intellectuals were not alone in determining the relations of French Catholics with politics and the state. The labor unions, both of industrial workers and of farmers, also played a decisive part in this connection.

The war had led the traditionally divided unions to band together against the German Occupation. The Communist-dominated CGT and the Catholic CFTC* published a joint manifesto in 1940, and worked together in the Resistance. But after the Liberation, the CGT threw its lot in with the Communist party, rode to victory with it, and shared its isolation (after an internal split which brought about the formation of another union, close to the Socialist party, the Force ouvrière).

* Confédération française des Travailleurs chrétiens (French Confederation of Christian Workers).

The Catholics who inclined to progressisme joined or collaborated with the CGT. They considered its Marxist analysis of French society accurate, and also approved of its nondenominational character; the Catholic union seemed to perpetuate the fusion of the Church and secular society. The CFTC itself was torn by dissensions and contradictions. A confederation of workers, it had originally been formed by salaried employees, but its character was changing as the manual workers became more numerous. It was a Catholic group, but it was not run by priests. Within the union there was a struggle between those who accepted the idea of class warfare and partisans of the corporate state, between the traditionalism of the Catholic social movement and the actual experiences of the workers.

Instead of disappearing, however, the CFTC enjoyed a remarkable growth. Influenced by intellectuals from the public-school teachers' union,* the SGEN (*Syndicat général de l'éducation nationale*), and also by the building- and steel-workers' union, it played a prominent part in strikes, was at least as aggressive as the CGT, and seemed more independent. Anarchist and libertarian influence—both schools have left their mark on French trade-unionism— explains why a trade union free of allegiance to any political party could stand comparison with the huge CGT, which was too closely tied to the Communists. As the membership of the CFTC increased in number, those who constituted a minority in the late forties now assumed the leadership of the union without causing any drastic upheaval. They had become the majority, and were accepted as such by the whole membership.

The new CFTC was made up of former JOC members. They had chosen it rather than the CGT at a time when a choice was still possible, immediately after the war. Their

---

* There was a separate union for teachers in private schools. (Trans.)

behavior epitomized the transformation of French Catholics, refusing to give their allegiance to any party, and specifically to the middle-of-the-road MRP, and came out in support of a "modern" and "democratic" socialism in 1953:

Our group was founded seven years ago by manual and intellectual workers, all militant trade-unionists, who were determined not to let their organization become subservient to any party, and equally determined to demand whatever is necessary for effective labor action.

We consider that a renewal of the French Left ranks first among these conditions. As we see the new French Left, it will be democratic, secular and socialist.

Democratic, of course, and antitotalitarian: transformation of the economic structures would be useless if unaccompanied by respect for, and the promotion of, the liberties that traditionally go together: political freedom, freedom of organization, and spiritual freedom.

This new French Left will necessarily be secular, since it holds that the state must be independent of all religious persuasions, respectful of all forms of belief and of unbelief, and that it must insure to each and every citizen freedom of conscience and the right to be sincere. We blame the authors of the Barangé law [giving government funds for Catholic schools] for establishing division in French public life along religious lines. We, on the contrary, want to erase this division among wage-earners in order to increase the forces of social change.

In order to master the coming national problems, the new Left must become specifically socialist. We cannot be content with some vague "social" spirit, but must change the function of investment capital, a matter of prime importance for an impoverished nation plagued with inadequate technical development, like France today. This function cannot be left, as traditional capitalism would have it, to the action of spontaneous savings and the free flow of money. Planning is necessary, and a policy of public invest- ments (which can be supported by taxation after a reform of the fiscal system) and of public control over private self- financing (which in fact constitutes indirect taxation).

The democratic state that will solve the vital problems of our country will be a socialist state, not only because it will acknowledge its responsibility for distributing national costs and redistributing revenues, but also because it will exercise control over the organization, transfer, and devel- opment of productive forces. . . .

Democratic Socialism must necessarily reinforce the ex- ercise of control by the people at the same time that it increases the managing powers of the state in the economic field. It is not enough to ensure the proper functioning of the institutions of political liberty; it will also be necessary to reawaken the spirit of these institutions—the spirit of control and of responsibility, which must, above all, be passed on from the citizen to the producer through the joint production committees. The latter could then assume the functions which we believe are theirs within the framework of an over-all economic collective response. The fate of democracy hangs on the technically revolutionary changes that must be made inside industrial enterprises.

That is the reason for our efforts to bring a number of key industries back to genuine trade-unionism, after years in which a totalitarian party and the organizations under its control have held sway over the workers.

In the course of this arduous conquest, which can be achieved only by sharing daily in the workers' struggles, the action of our comrades against the reactionary forces has often seemed to coincide with that of organizations belong- ing to the CGT. Ever since the end of 1948, we have deliberately considered concerted action with Stalinist unions when the labor situation required it as merely a unity of circumstances. We wanted to avoid what the Communist party wanted: the establishment of a common front through which militant non-Communist unionists would witness the dissolution of their own organizations and lose even their own identity.

In the fields of information and of education, our efforts have tended to impress on our members that peace as we want it, for instance, is not peace as the present CGT understands it, and that if we strive for an anticapitalist revolution, it is not the kind that the present CGT is trying to bring about.

In order to give perspectives regarding post-capitalist possibilities different from those offered by the Stalinists, we have devoted a considerable part of our efforts to information regarding developments in other countries—for example, in the British Labor party. That is also why (as well as for other reasons) we have deliberately rejected the "little Europe" sponsored by The Six,* which is nothing but a restoration of European capitalism under the cover of Christian democracy, and why we will not consider any organization of Western Europe itself to which the British and Scandinavian Labor parties could not agree.

Beyond the differences that may still result from divergent backgrounds, the multiplicity of organizations, ignorance and misunderstandings hitherto unavoidable in this or that sector, our basic premises lead us to carry out parallel or joint action. . . . [21]

Even if these words bear the imprint of a trend and of an era—even if, from 1958 on, the crisis which jointly affected

* France, Germany, Holland, Belgium, Luxembourg, and Italy.

socialism and industrial society compelled the Left to revise its analyses—even so, the CFTC, although it evolved, did not repudiate its principles. For instance, during the great debate carried on during the sixties over the mode of political action to be adopted by unionism (contention or participation), it refused to consider any form of integration of unionism into the state, but, shunning revolutionary romanticism, strove to define the conditions which should govern the participation of labor unions in a rational, deliberative, and contractual democracy.

Finally, the CFTC wished to be the organ of those Christians who exercised their responsibilities in a secular society; it was not only independent of the ecclesiastical authorities, but open to all (believers or unbelievers) who agreed with its thinking and its actions. Since the war, the minority (which later became the majority) had made no secret of the fact that it intended to delete the word "Christian" from the organization's title. It was no longer simply a question of drawing a distinction between temporal and spiritual matters, but of translating into deeds a new Christian concept of history.

Some, of course, felt that refusing to call the union "Christian" was a sign of radical "dechristianization." But those who supported the deletion were as firm Catholics as France had ever produced. They were not opportunists; they were not trying to entice workers who would not want to join the Church by getting them to join their labor union. They thought that the Church no longer had any need to increase the number of Christian institutions in order to carry out its mission. They were trying to make the world as God wanted it to be, and were thus going back to the great apostolic tradition and that primordial Christian desire of "restoring all things in Christ." All this presupposed respect for the truth of the world and a clear distinction between the mission of the Church and the exercise of governmental power.

The new synthesis had not yet been elaborated. The majority of Christians had not gone beyond the discovery that politics had a realm of its own, that faith must be extricated from a tangle of superfluous compromises. But it was only a stage on the road. The spirit of the Gospel had to make a new alliance with political know-how.

Changes in Rural Life

City, country: it was only yesterday that these words evoked two worlds that were entirely alien to each other. But the rural population (for the change was affecting the whole of it, not only the farmers) were becoming full-fledged citizens of the new industrial society, and Christians played a leading role in this development.

It all sprang from the fundamental discovery that our traditional agricultural society was dying; to build a new society was a pressing necessity. Abbé Boulard analyzed the problem:

We have been living for eleven centuries on the strength of an agricultural and Christian society which created fine local Christian communities. It was a world of small craftsmen and family-centeredness in alliance with the Church. It was a simple life without great needs, but somewhat restricted by parish or district boundaries. At its best such a culture produced men and women whose charity was tactful and conscience unwavering. . . .

It is quite understandable that our love for the past—especially in view of what that past gave to parish life and what were its Christian achievements—should awaken in us a nostalgic longing for the only form of Christian rural civilization which we have actually ever known, and that the main pastoral concern of many priests should be, as it has always been, to save the old ways at any cost.

But the time has come for us to see how childish this is. In this area, the war of 1939, like that of 1914, has made us a generation older.

In the course of our survey, we found some magnificent specimens of Christian communities of the old style, where charity and conscience remain.

But to our dismay, we found that all were fatally doomed.

Either, although "well-preserved," they are dying in situ, like Pierrefiche-du-Larzac in Aveyron, where the population has fallen from 220 inhabitants in 1880 to 90 now, these 90 including sixteen unmarried people over thirty years old; where not one marriage has occurred in eleven years (between December 1932 and December 1943), and two-thirds of the families will become extinct for lack of descendants.

Or, the population is old, as at Salles-la-Source in the same administrative district, where the number of inhabitants dwindled from 652 to 380 in fifty years and where the birth rate has reached the extraordinarily low figure of 8.8 per thousand.

Or again, if the parishes are alive, their ways are changing. Consider the place in Lorraine, for instance, where "in spite of every effort made to preserve ancestral traditions, the young—particularly the men—are going along with the times. They still obey, but the reasons for the rules must be explained to them. Both the young men and the girls are avid for movies, outings, a free and independent life. Young men are sports enthusiasts, especially for soccer, and will bicycle some ten to thirteen miles to play in a match or watch a game."

We must loyally recognize that the stream of life is bypassing our old rural Christian communities: either they are changing and taking on a new look, or else they are dying of old age within their own enclaves, like the "dead cities" of the Rhone delta, which the river left to decay when it changed its course. . . .

The old civilization of our peasantry constituted a Christianizing element of considerable strength: in human terms it seems that where it is still alive, people save their souls much more easily than elsewhere.

But this civilization is finished: the young are through with it, and an exodus toward the towns, greater than the one we witnessed before the war, is now developing in the villages.

Our real problem, therefore, is to succeed in establishing a new rural civilization, a modern society with a highly developed economic and social life, which will also be as radically Christian as its forerunner. This is the only effort that makes sense.[22]

The rural crisis is a matter of concern to all believers. Peasant Christendom—around its village churches, submissive to nature rather than dominating it, worshipping God in his works rather than doing his work, lagging behind the "modern" intellectual and social revolution—had long been the model for Christian behavior. For the Church, the death of traditional rural society was as great an event as the murder of the king had been to the political society of the eighteenth century. . . . The rapprochement between industrial and farm workers was an expression in economic terms of a situation that also had its religious aspects.

But men and women were needed to take matters in hand. They existed, too, largely because rural Catholic Action had trained them. The Church was not caught un-

awares, as it had been by the first Industrial Revolution.
Young Christians were to overwhelm other political forces
in farm areas—including Socialists and Communists. On
economic grounds, they argued for structural reforms
rather than guaranteed minimum prices; in other words,
they were not asking for aid but wanted to be responsible
for their own "revolution." Former members of *Jeunesse
agricole chrétienne* and the *Mouvement familial rural* were
in the foreground of rural trade-unionism. The new farm
leaders were very much like the leaders of other social
groups.

*Although they were not ignorant of the preceding pe-
riod, the young were inclined to take the Occupation years
as a starting point for their analyses. . . .* But, because of
various political developments, a multiplicity of agricultural organizations arose. The socialist trend had come to
rest in the permanent quarters of the radicals: the Confédération nationale de la Mutualité, du Crédit et de la Coopéra-
tion agricole (National Confederation of Mutual Insurance
and Loan Societies and of Agricultural Co-operatives);
that was their "Boulevard St. Germain." The "rural inde-
pendents" were to be found rather with the FNSEA** and
the Agriculture Chambers which had disappeared in 1940,
but had come back as early as November 1948, and had
begun to function once more in 1950.*
   However, something had happened: new organizations
had been created and there were new trends abroad. . . .
The study centers answered the taste of the young for

* See the unsigned article, "Une nouvelle race de paysans," *Témoignage
chrétien*, January 27, 1961.
   ** *Fédération nationale des Syndicats d'Exploitants Agricoles* (National
Federation of Agricultural Producers).

group research and a more scientific approach to farming. . . .

From 1954 to 1957, various factors led the Young Farmers' Clubs Association to revise its mission and its tasks. On March 8, 1957, in the course of a "historic" 'General Assembly, the nature of the association was changed. . . . Its purpose was now to protect the interests of young agricultural producers.*

Trained by the JAC, the young elements of the rural world leaned toward these organizations. They could express themselves better and be more efficient in them than in the institutions set up by the preceding generation. Hitherto, they had been able to speak only through their fathers who, as heads of an agricultural enterprise, were alone entitled to membership in a union. Contrary to the prevailing custom in other branches of the economy, the agricultural worker who was neither the head of an agricultural enterprise nor a wage earner, could influence the development of history only through intermediaries. Several millions of persons had thus been reduced to obscurity and silence, and some of them were among the most active in the world of agriculture: the sons and daughters, the wives, brothers and sisters of "the head". . . . This silence was about to be broken, no easy feat and one that did not go without arousing the suspicion of those who had become so used to speaking and hearing themselves speak, with never an echo or a partner to answer back. As Mr. Estrangin had expressed it during the Semaine sociale held at Reims in 1961, we had gone from a democracy by delegation to "a democracy founded on participation. . . ."[23]

---

* *Témoignage chrétien*, March 15, 1957, p. 7.

VI

The Struggle Against Colonialism

The Beginnings of Protest

France emerged from World War II poorly prepared to understand the immense aspiration to independence of colonized peoples. For years Frenchmen had complacently assumed that they were bringing progress and civilization to the unenlightened; with their memories of the Occupation so recent, it was impossible for them to take seriously the idea that they, in their turn, might be oppressors. An additional factor was de Gaulle's reliance on the overseas territories in developing the concept of "Free France" at a time when France itself was paralyzed. Everything tended to confirm Frenchmen in their belief that they had a vocation as colonizers, in the manner of the Romans.

At its outset, the war in Indochina was run by a government which included Communists, and which actually represented the vast majority of Frenchmen in the euphoria of Liberation. When the Algerian uprisings in 1945 were answered by repressive violence against the Moslems of Kabylia, there were almost no protests; even the Communist papers did not mention it. Soon, however, the breakup of the Resistance coalition encouraged greater attention to be given to developments in Indochina. The Communists began a protest campaign, and *Témoignage chrétien, Esprit,* and the *Bulletin des chrétiens progressistes* denounced the war in Indochina as an unjust undertaking, and one that could not succeed.

In general, French Catholics were no better prepared than their compatriots for the trial of decolonization. Before the war, their horizon was almost completely limited to Europe; beyond was nothing but an immense expanse to be civilized and baptized. But the claims of the colonized peoples soon began to affect Christian consciences; implicitly or explicitly, the political crisis raised the question of Christian universalism. The issue was whether the different peoples of the world were to have the right to organize their own nations and cultures. If, after many debates, the majority of Catholics supported decolonization, it was because the spirit of the Gospel required it.

Nevertheless, few were prepared to advocate independence. Since they blamed "nationalism" for two world wars, they preferred to talk in terms of "international communities," and were attracted to the official idea of a "French union," which did not allow the peoples who composed it the prior right of choice. Although a growing number of Catholics sincerely desired the transformation of the Empire, they did not yet see the necessity, or the price, of complete decolonization.

It should be recalled that it was mostly the Catholic representatives of the MRP who, with the Socialists, shared responsibility for colonial affairs, and firmly opposed all efforts at negotiation with the Viet-Minh. It was the Communists who took the lead in the struggle against colonialism, and a Communist sailor, Henri Martin, became a symbol of their effort when he was arrested in 1950 for distributing tracts calling on soldiers to refuse to fight against the Vietnamese. Martin defended himself courageously before a military court, but was given a five-year sentence. Some Catholics took up his defense, and Jean-Marie Domenach used the occasion to pose the problem of military insubordination for motives of conscience:

The soldier is not tied to the army by a special act of nature which would affect his personality, but retains his fundamental rights. The laws of the army have the same substance as other laws. Military authority is not above other authorities; in a republic like ours, it is subordinate to civil authority. Hence the right of revolt remains substantially intact, even if its expression is more difficult and involves greater risks. This is particularly clear to Catholics, who recognize the obligation in certain cases of disobeying the Pope himself, although for them he represents an authority of a much higher order than any secular one, civil or military. . . . The freedom to refuse an order does not disappear upon entering a military camp. If it did, why would the Church place on its altars so many saints who refused to bear arms? Is there not even greater reason to praise those who, while being in the army, refuse to participate in a war which violates their conscience?

On this point the Christian spirit is in accord with the international court at Nuremberg, which refused to accept military discipline as an adequate defense, and offered as a principle that no one can execute an order in support of genocide or a crime against humanity. Since we reproach so many German soldiers for having passively followed military orders, should we not have a prejudice in favor of a French soldier who refuses to be the accomplice of an unjust war? Even the old Prussian military code specified that disobedience to orders was permitted when they infringed on the Ten Commandments. Have we fallen below this ancient military tradition, and shall we refuse a French soldier that freedom of conscience we constantly invoke to explain the basis of democracy, and which, only a few years ago, was the source of our resistance to Hitler?[1]

Meanwhile, North Africa was in ferment. In Tunisia decisive reforms were delayed until 1954; in Morocco there was stern repression; the French administration wanted to get rid of the nationalist party and the Sultan, Mohammed V. In a slum district of Casablanca dozens of poor people were massacred by the police in December, 1952. A few priests and some members of the Little Brothers of Jesus, along with intellectuals and social workers, alerted their coreligionists in France. A meeting was organized by Robert Barrat at the Centre catholique des Intellectuels français, and *Témoignage chrétien* published a long report on Morocco in its issue of April 10, 1953. François Mauriac, who had previously defended "Western civilization" in his column for the conservative *Figaro*, was overwhelmed by the weight of evidence, and launched a passionate protest. In his "Bloc-Notes" for *L'Express*, he made a special point of attacking those Catholic politicians who were among the principal artisans of colonial repression:

It is a bitter thought that this criminal and inept record, which for ten years has been written in blood, was made by Christians, by those whose coming to power after the Lib-

eration filled me with joy and pride. We must have the courage to admit it: ten years later, the failure of Christian Democracy has equaled the failure of integral nationalism.

In my opinion the Christian Democrats in office have betrayed their vocation, which was to make clear that politics was not outside the moral law. Once they were in power, the men of the MRP exploded this truth, precisely at the moment when they had a chance to give a proof of it—and when, if I may say so, history was on God's side, since in Indochina, Morocco, and Tunisia, political truth is justice.[2]

In June 1953, under the presidency of Mauriac, a committee was founded for a just peace in North Africa; its guiding spirit was another Catholic who had been preaching respect for Arabs for forty years: Louis Massignon, professor at the Collège de France and a renowned Islamic scholar. He had an intense sense of the sacred; he constantly bore witness to the importance of keeping one's word, protecting the poor and the oppressed, and practicing nonviolence. A friend of the finest minds of Islam, Massignon also regularly visited North African prisoners and was the confidant of innumerable young Moslems. Massignon did not take a political position, but appealed to the fundamental solidarity of believers, both Christians and Moslems. For him this "common honor of faith" was the foundation of a policy of total decolonization:

To make use of human language, to bring evidence, or to speak in the name of God purely as a propaganda tactic, a profitable bluff, is very tempting for militarists and profiteers who think only of immediate results. But war and its devices must give way to peace, for which diplomacy is demanded, seeking with the adversary (who now has become an interlocutor) a dialogue that will be something *other than a bluff. It then becomes necessary to try to understand this other speaker in terms of what is best in him, in his testimony as a believer, even and especially if we no longer believe. He must not be corrupted or used for our own dubious purposes. Instead of imposing, in the name of our cultural superiority, our most questionable methods of getting rich, perhaps we might be able to recover, by contact with this "backward" Moroccan Moslem, the sense of the sacred. We might begin with the notion of the right of asylum, that generous hospitality which allowed us to come and establish ourselves in his home, and which would permit us to remain there, provided we have not finally disgusted him.*[3]

From this point French Catholics—particularly intellectuals and those active in the labor movement—took a growing part in the struggle against colonialism, a part which was to become more important than that of the Communists. In most areas there were violent crises; in black Africa, because the French population was small, the evolution was smoother. In 1953 the French bishops of West Africa published a statement which recognized in principle the legitimacy of the right to independence. The bishops in Madagascar had done the same just previously. In addition, a series of administrative and social reforms tended to give the African territories a growing autonomy. There is a striking contrast between the policy practiced with these poor countries and that maintained toward such relatively rich countries as Vietnam and Algeria.

The Algerian War

The Algerian Revolt began in 1954 with an uprising of mountain tribesmen on November first. Shortly afterward, representatives of the various youth groups in Algeria—

including the leaders of Catholic Action and the Scout movement—wrote the Governor-General to express their concern regarding reprisals, arbitrary arrests, the use of torture, and the execution of prisoners. The Algerian nationalists stepped up their campaign of terrorism, and in response, "pacification" became even more savage. Among the young officers recalled for service in Algeria, Jean Muller, a Catholic Scout leader, was shocked by what he saw, and described the torture practices employed by the French in letters to his friends. After Muller himself was killed in an ambush, his letters were published in *Témoignage chrétien*, causing a crisis of conscience for those Catholics who were alarmed that the French army could be responsible for such atrocities.* Unfortunately the French bishops were slow in denouncing these practices, and after "regretting some shameful acts," their statement (October 14, 1955) went on to warn against "unfair generalizations." A violent campaign was soon unleashed against those who were attacking the honor of the army and aiding the enemies of France; Henri Marrou protested against this exploitation of patriotism in an article in *Le Monde* (April 5, 1956):

I am being asked to help maintain the "French presence" in North Africa. Therefore, I have the sovereign duty of asking myself if this presence has been, and is today, authentically French. France is not France if she is unfaithful to the ideal image which she set out to incarnate. . . . As a theologian, I learned from my master, St. Augustine, a Berber, that all nations are necessarily a mixture, which it is not impossible for us to disentangle, of the City of Good and the City of Evil. But theology, history, and good sense have also taught me that those civilizations

* See Chapter 3, pp. 96–97.

which have allowed a gulf to develop between the ideal they invoke and the realization of it that they offer end by dying of hypocrisy. . . .

Marrou and others—both Catholics and Protestants—formed a Comité de Résistance spirituelle which published a collection of documents on the atrocities; the response from officers—and sometimes priests—was that "order must be maintained." A Catholic writer, Pierre-Henri Simon, attacked precisely this kind of justification in a powerful pamphlet:

At the home of a friend, I happened to meet a Catholic chaplain who had just returned from Indochina, seriously wounded. He was a fine-looking young man, an active priest and courageous Frenchman. Because of my concern, I asked him if there was any truth in these stories about torture. His answer was calm, "Yes, it's true; it's inevitable in the kind of war we face over there." He saw me begin to protest, and went on: "Look, think for a minute. Suppose you were in the thick of the jungle, in charge of a section, with your buddies behind you. The Viets are all around, but invisible. You've got to know what they're concocting, where they're waiting for you; it's a matter of life and death for the forty Frenchmen. Well, if you had a chance to learn what you needed to know by arresting a village woman and driving a nail through her hand until she talked, would you hesitate? No, and you would be right." I was shaken by his attitude, but then thought perhaps my reaction was too much that of an intellectual, far removed from the field of action. Finally, I realized that my first response was right. . . . The strength of principles is that they are principles—expressions of an absolute that no consideration of circumstances or self-interest can destroy. We must be circumspect in judging the actions of another; God alone knows

*the degree of guilt of the French officer who nails the hand
of a Vietnamese woman, like the centurion who, also under
orders, nailed the hand of Christ. But we must remain firm
in our moral evaluation of the act: what is evil can never
be good. If soldiers who have used torture for what they
consider their duty in a given situation tell me, "In our
place you would have done the same," I can only answer,
"That's possible, but if I did, I know I would be doing
wrong." We are collectively guilty and France is in a state
of sin if Frenchmen do not protest against the adoption of
ignoble practices which are contrary to the principle of
that civilization which they are pretending to maintain.*[4]

1957 and 1958 were years of constant challenge and
inner torment in France. Elections produced a new government controlled by the Front Republicain, and led by a
Socialist, Guy Mollet. In February 1956 Mollet had
yielded to the intimidation of a mob of French *colons* in
Algiers; in practice his government left all power to the
army in Algeria. General Massu took over responsibility
for maintaining order at the beginning of 1957; the terrorism of Algerian nationalists was met by the ruthless
repression of French parachutists. Even in France the government tried to silence all those who questioned these
methods; newspapers were seized, and there were constant
threats and arrests. For Christians the problem was to take
a clear position without being led to justify one violence
against another, staying close to reality, and not taking
refuge in lofty statements of principle.

The Witness of Priests

As the tragedy deepened, the situation of an increasing
number of priests became more and more difficult. Some

who had been recalled for service in the army sent letters and eyewitness statements which were organized in a report used by Cardinal Feltin in his intervention with the government. A letter addressed by thirty-five priest-officers to their bishops, which appeared in the papers in April 1959, summarized their impossible role: "We are caught between the solidarity which links us with our fighting comrades and the proclamation of the Gospel which is our fundamental concern."

On the other hand, years of camaraderie and the tradition of close relations between the Church and the army led the vast majority of military chaplains to share the point of view of their superior officers. Many young Catholics complained that the Church was leaving them without clear directives or moral assistance as they confronted the problems involved in the "pacification" of Algeria.

In Algeria itself the European population, which consisted of almost a million people, considered itself a Catholic minority in a Moslem country, a dominant minority even though principally composed of people who were not well-to-do. The latent racism of the Europeans was only inflamed by the nationalist insurrection, and, unfortunately, most priests identified with "their own kind"; they did not look on themselves as Christ's witnesses in an Islamic land, but as defenders of Christendom under attack. A letter from Abbé Bérenguer, a parish priest of Oran (where a military court sentenced him to prison in 1959), emphasized the frightening responsibility of the clergy:

They have not taught, by word and example, the practical requirements of Christianity in this country; they have not waged the necessary life-and-death struggle with the rampant racism, and as a group they now find themselves contaminated to the point of forgetting in practice the most

elementary ideas of Christianity. By turning their backs on
the Gospel, how could they hope to build Christianity in
this European milieu? How would Our Lord have permitted it? . . .

I know that all proselytism was forbidden by the Colonial Office. And the French priest, who, as everyone
knows, is a good patriot, has obeyed this regulation to the
point of completely ignoring Islam, not even taking a good
look at it. He speaks and acts as if he were simply a member of the French clergy, forgetting that he is supposed to
be a priest of the Church and of all men. He believes he is
abstaining from all politics, but in fact his silence is that of
an accomplice and his culpable inaction becomes simply
bad politics. . . .

"The only error and one tragedy in the world," Bernanos said, "is not knowing how to love." This has been the
great tragedy in this country for more than a hundred
years. Christians have not known how to love. The clergy
has not known how to love. Let us confess, and ask pardon
of the Lord, and do reparation. The Church is missionary
or it has no being—in Algeria as elsewhere. Missions
should have been established here a hundred years ago;
Rome asked for them in vain. Instead, dioceses were established on the same basis as in France, and the Colonial
Office made it clear to the clergy that they were there
exclusively to take care of Europeans.

The Mission de France had established several communities in Algeria. Their reports to the hierarchy on the situation of the Algerians, both in France and in Algeria,
called on the Church to break its silence. Three priests of
the Mission de France had already been expelled from
Algeria in 1956, despite the protests of the Bishop of Constantine and of Cardinal Liénart; they were "guilty" of

offering aid and assistance to the sick and the wounded, and of attempting to bring Arabs and Europeans together in a common prayer for peace. Archbishop Duval of Algiers continued to affirm the demands of conscience, condemning the use of dishonorable means of maintaining order, and recommending greater efforts toward "fraternal dialogue."

Even in France a difficult problem was presented to priests who were assigned to working-class districts where they could see for themselves the conditions in which 400,-000 Algerian workers were living in various French cities. One of these priests, Abbé Carteron, was accused by the police of having worked for the FLN, and wrote an open letter to his fellow priests of the diocese of Lyons:

In the parish where I was stationed in 1948, there were about 3,000 Algerians living in material and moral destitution. At the time, I had no idea of the Algerian problem, and went along with the other priests of the parish, trying to be of help by teaching them French, starting a night school, looking for apartments, trying to help them make friends with French people in the neighborhood, and so forth.

It soon became clear that there was an immense work to be done, and that in order to do it, we would have to get to know them better, which would involve learning their language, their culture, their suffering and aspirations. What we had been doing was too superficial.

I tried to learn Arabic, but simply did not have enough time free from parish duties; for a while I even tried to forget about the misery that persisted within the confines of the parish. A year later, without my asking or wanting it, His Eminence, conscious of his role as bishop, gave me a specific mission: "There are in my diocese 30,000 Moslems for whom I have responsibility before God, since they

are my guests. No one seems to be thinking of them. Will
you share this responsibility with me? I confide their care to
you; do what you can. Before God, we do not have the
right to ignore them."

I posed only one condition: "Before taking on such a
problem, it is important that I get to understand it
well. Let me have two years to become informed."

I then made a clean sweep of everything I knew, except
the Gospel and theology, and went humbly to the school of
this new world. Since then, I have considered myself the
Church's delegate among the Arabs. One incident will help
explain my attitude. After two years of travel in North
Africa, studying, learning Arabic, becoming familiar with
Moslem theology and African customs, I took a job as a
sweeper with a group of Arab workers in order to understand their life of poverty better. After a month, an official
in the Prefecture of Constantine, learning who I was, had
me thrown off the job and expelled from the village where I
was living, because—as he told the Vicar General of the
area—"That priest has no right to get familiar with Arabs
like he does unless he is a police spy."

That same day, when my companions—who did not
know I was a priest—learned that I had been fired, one of
them said to me confidentially, "Will you tell us who you
are? In spite of the instinctive confidence we have had in
you, we have constantly asked ourselves whether you were
a police spy. Now we know you're not, but where have you
come from?"

I answered, "I am a sort of spy, but not for the police—I
am a kind of agent for . . . God! My religious chief at
Lyons told me, 'There are many North African workers
among us; we have the sacred duty of hospitality, whose
first requirement is to get to know them. Go, then, to their

country, and see what's going on; study their problems. Then come back and tell us about things.' "

My comrade embraced me, and thanked me. . . .

When I returned to Lyons, the question of what to do for these 30,000 Arab workers still remained. They were usually given the hardest and dirtiest jobs; ninety per cent were illiterate; the vast majority were living in slum housing.

Because of my travels, I was also aware of the 700,000 heads of families in Algeria who had never found jobs, and their hungry, half-naked children; and I had been brought to realize that their material destitution was less cruel than their psychological impoverishment, their lack of dignity. Ultimately, the 30,000 Algerian workers in the Lyons area had forced me to consider twenty million Moslems in North Africa, and their four hundred million coreligionists in Africa, the Near East, and the Far East; these in turn were part of the world's billion and a half (and still growing) "underdeveloped" population. . . .

As I took up my work again in Lyons, I realized that my job was to keep Christians informed about their North African brothers working all around them, and at the same time to remain close to these workers—not preaching to them, but listening to them, getting to understand them. Parallel with this double task, I had another attitude which I believe should be that of every Catholic chaplain.

What is a priest to do when his Bishop says to him, "I am putting you in charge of the students," or "I want you to work with the farmers"? First of all, he should get to know the particular milieu—its main points of strength, its natural groupings, its deep aspirations, and the ideal toward which Providence seems to be directing it. He should build on its dynamic and healthy elements, and remember the effectiveness of like working with like. . . .

I have tried to keep these ideas before me in my work,

and for years have been able to get to know the finest of these Algerian workers. When they met one who was generous, dedicated, fraternal, and loyal, they introduced him to me, and I tried to put him in touch with like-minded young Frenchmen. When I recently refused to introduce one of them to a Catholic youth group, since he was not up to the ideal I had of an Algerian, they said to me, "What's the matter? Do you want us all to be saints?" "That's right," I answered; "I have too high an opinion of you to be willing to act otherwise."

I have never argued religion with my Algerian friends; as for politics, I was by their side as a man of God, regardless of their political choices. . . . I am aware that some thought I should not associate with these people, because they were "anti-French." What they told me themselves, however, was that "It is not France as such that we hate, but an unjust regime." Even if they were "anti-French," the Church, we must remember, is supranational. . . .

What am I accused of?

The report which led to my ouster from North Africa mentioned "contacts with nationalists; encourages Algerians to organize."

A year ago a police inspector reproached me for having an Algerian worker live at my home for more than a year; after leaving Lyons, this man became a leader. . . .

I gave encouragement to the efforts of some young Algerians to provide a genuine Social Security program for workers who were held in custody, their families and children; I also helped them find a center. If I had asked them what political group they belonged to before doing them this service, I would have been leaving my role as a priest and been doing what I was accused of—"mixing in politics."

I found a place to live for some married students. . . .

In fact, I have merely been following the principles given me by my Superiors:

1) to aid—morally, spiritually, and materially—all Algerians in their human needs (housing, food, employment, and so forth) without concerning myself with their ideas or organizational activities;

2) to refuse categorically any assistance in political matters, and above all, any collaboration in acts of violence. . . .

Other priests of the Mission de France were arrested for having aided the FLN, or "encouraging insubordination and desertion." There were new protests and demonstrations, but police raids continued, and thousands of militants were jailed. On October 17, 1961, the FLN organized a demonstration in Paris in which 50,000 Algerians marched in the street. The Paris police, remembering that some of its own men had been killed by nationalists, committed a ferocious act of repression. Hundreds were rushed into concentration camps, and about seventy were executed. The CFTC immediately published a white paper on police atrocities, and for an increasing number of Catholics, priests and laymen, speaking out became an obsession. It would be impossible to list all the speeches, sermons, manifestoes, articles, pamphlets, and books; but even though many publications were banned, the police were rarely able to confiscate them, since they were usually distributed by loyal militants, and in this way the truth about the Algerian War was still available in France.

The Scandal of Conscience

The soldier's moral problem was probably the most difficult. If he wished to bear witness, he put himself in opposition to his milieu and to the traditional rule of military

obedience; he also faced more serious penalties than the
journalist or civilian intellectual. A young Catholic Lieutenant, Jean Le Meur, was the first to bring this issue into
the open. His letters, published in *Esprit*, constitute one of
the most moving documents of the Algerian War, register-
ing the scandal of a Christian conscience obstructed in its
desire to act in accordance with its principles.

Le Meur wrote the following letter to the Minister of
National Defense on July 6, 1958:

Honorable and dear Sir:

*I have the honor to inform you of my deliberate refusal
to serve in Algeria in the operations now being undertaken
to maintain order. Consequently, I beg you to accept my
resignation from the rank of lieutenant, and I hold myself
available at your convenience for all sanctions which I
have incurred because of my indiscipline.*

*By accepting the command of a platoon, I would be
helping to put down a revolt which has good reason to
exist, and of defeating rebels whose cause I cannot in conscience condemn.*

*Colonel Marey, Commandant at the Ecole Militaire at
Cherchell, flatly disavowed my action, and has sharply
reproached me for a lack of honesty and courage in avoiding the problem for so long. I realize that before accepting
the rank of officer I should have weighed more maturely
the duties which this would entail.*

*Despite my insubordination, I beg you, sir, to accept the
expression of my very respectful deference, and to believe
in my complete devotion to the service of France.*

Lieutenant Le Meur was sent into action, having
received no response to this letter, and wrote to his parents
from Algeria on August 29:

Dear parents,

I would like to answer Father's objections, since it is important for me to justify my action to you; I very much want the support of my own home.

I recognize that the traditional morality of the Church would maintain that man does not bear full moral responsibility for those actions which the laws of society impose on him. This is true when it is a matter of excusing Christians who participate in undertakings that sometimes deserve to be condemned. But can we say that a German, who had become aware of what Nazism implied and was in fact accomplishing, was bound by obedience to the laws of his nation? On the contrary, I think he was morally bound to reject them. I am not saying there is a perfect parallel; I hope that the Algerian War is less terrible, but I believe that it is fundamentally wrong. If casuists should authorize me, in the interests of national solidarity, to help in perpetrating a crime, the casuists would be wrong. In an ambiguous situation, a man may reserve his judgment and hold on to the benefit of the doubt. In this situation, there is no possible doubt for me. I must seize the opportunity to refuse.

For a long time the Church has tried to reassure the conscience of the faithful who were involved in difficult situations by telling them, "Don't worry; you're not responsible. Your leaders will decide." This amounts to saying that on certain occasions, we are allowed to be irresponsible automatons. But a man can never pass his responsibility on to someone else. In the last recourse, it is the one who executes an action who decides. Of course, such an attitude is in some respects a negative rejection, breaking solidarity with a community, but it is also the affirmation of the permanence of moral responsibility, of solidarity with other disinherited peoples, and of the possibility of an ultimate dialogue.

I took part in a week-long operation between Seiar, Guentis and Taberdga. . . . Over the radio, we heard the unit commander repeat: "I don't want any prisoners." Victims were thrown from the height of a cliff into the wadi. People spoke of keeping some prisoners "to get information." Villages were completely destroyed; populations were "regrouped"—how is this different from deportation? . . .

For the moment, my life is not disagreeable. The Commandant is a gentleman; I get along with my men, whom I will regret leaving. I am getting a tan and eat well. I've been paid, so I'm quite rich, and nothing would prevent me from fighting this war if I didn't have to lie to myself constantly. . . .

Even if one gets a soft job in headquarters, communications, or supply, one is part of a machine of repression, and responsible. What I have discovered, precisely, is the permanence of individual responsibility in a system which pretends to abolish it.

Soon after, Le Meur was arrested for openly disapproving of an officer's order not to take prisoners. He continued his testimony in a letter to a friend on September 17:

Yesterday evening at ten o'clock I heard shrieks in a nearby barracks, and went out to see. It was what you think—an "interrogation." A dozen police were watching the spectacle from outside. I don't know what method they were using; I think it was electricity. I remained about ten seconds and left after expressing my disgust. The séance lasted for more than an hour. Until then, I knew this sort of thing went on, but now there remain within me those terrible shrieks which end in childish sobs.

Nevertheless, the torturers resemble us and are often good company. They regret "the unfortunate necessities of war which are imposed on us. But we have to protect men's lives, and besides, these individuals probably had many crimes on their consciences." They reproach me for having given aid to the Communists. The room where the questioning took place was right on the street; on the other side are Moslem houses, and the groans of the prisoners could easily be heard two hundred feet away. . . .

Here it is dangerous to say that there are things that one does not do. Reading the military regulations will end up becoming an act of subversion. I am still shaken by the terrible revelation of yesterday. Nevertheless, there is worse, if I can believe G. and some others. What is going on ought to make it impossible for anyone to sleep, but the protests, even of the Left, have been very mild. Nevertheless, I believe that my protest, however isolated and fugitive, may be able to bear fruit. But it is a small hope. . . .

I write badly and with little order. I dream of having long, frivolous conversations. Péguy and the Psalms have been a great help to me. Prayer, which we so easily neglect when everything is going along well, becomes the only recourse, and there grows the desire for perfection.

Yesterday too I had the terrible feeling that in this tragic hour my friendships would not succeed in dissolving a compact solitude. We will need each other.

Le Meur was given a two-year sentence; there were others in Algeria who refused obedience, and some in France refused to return to Algeria or even to put on the uniform. The question then was raised whether conscientious objection should become a platform, capable of rallying a large number of young soldiers.

Francis Jeanson, an existentialist writer who had organ-

ized "a network of assistance for the FLN," in which a
good number of Catholics and even some priests were
included, advocated refusal to register, desertion, and aid
to the Algerian nationalists. However, the majority of the
Catholic Left, as well as the leaders of Catholic Action,
rejected this extreme attitude. For them, peace in Algeria
could result only from compromise; civil war would only
provoke army intervention, a seizure of power by a military fascism, and a prolongation of the war. Since the military coup at Algiers in May 1958, General de Gaulle had
taken over the government. Some thought he was a prisoner of those who were plotting to "keep Algeria French,"
and should be bitterly attacked (this was the position of
Sartre); others, that he was a realist who was preparing for
negotiations with the FLN by indirect routes; for a third
group he was a pragmatist who was waiting for the right
time to make his choice.

Several years passed in this uncertainty. The aggravation
of the repression in Algeria and the immobility of the
Gaullist government drove some young intellectuals to co-
operate with the nationalists. At the same time, there developed another center of resistance: the nonviolent, who
were grouped around Lanza del Vasto, a Sicilian whose
patron was Gandhi. Del Vasto, a kind of prophet of Christian nonviolence, had founded a community in southern
France that lived off the land. In the beginning of 1960
some of his young disciples decided to share the fate of the
five thousand Algerians who had been held without trial in
internment camps. They appeared at the gates of these
camps as "volunteers," accompanied by demonstrators who
marched in silence. One of these marches in April 1960
brought together a thousand Parisians at the camp at
Vincennes, including many Catholic intellectuals and a
number of priests. They were arrested by the police, led

into tunnels, and released in the middle of the night, far from Paris. This only led to further silent demonstrations whose slogan was: "We are all suspects."

The thirty nonviolent "volunteers" were arrested ten times, but continued their effort, leaving their families and their jobs, and living in solidarity. They would sit silently in front of prisoners or before the offices of government ministers; each time they would be led away by the police, and released in some deserted spot.

Toward the end of 1960, eleven of these volunteers decided to surround a young man who refused to go to Algeria—Jacques Muir. They all tore up their identity papers and, chained to each other on a public square in Paris, cried out with one voice that they were each Jacques Muir. They were put in jail, and it took the police several weeks before they could discover their real identity. Jo Pyronnet —to whom the police had given the name X12, and who was in fact the group's organizer—wrote the following letter from prison:

X12 *calling himself Jacques Muir*   *Christmas Eve, 1960*
No. 51 125   *La Santé Prison*
10–20
Dear Master,

Thank you for your letter of the twenty-first. It's the only one I've gotten the first week I've been here. . . .

Needless to say, I am not asking you to state that I am or am not Jacques Muir. That's not the problem. Jacques Muir was going to be arrested December 15, in accordance with the law; he offered himself with his comrades for arrest on that day. This application of the law seems unjust, but we accept it since it is legal, and demand its rigorous enforcement for all twelve. When a truth is so demanding that it places in question the very meaning of your life, you cannot accept that it be hidden under a bushel. This is the meaning of that comedy (or liturgy) of our being chained together: to give our act the character of a public testimony, so that the problem is posed and everyone is able to make a judgment on it in his own soul. This is also the meaning of each of us saying: "I refuse to have any other identity than that of Jacques Muir."

Power and justice close their eyes and ears, for fear of understanding. They knew the real identity of most of us; we are not part of an underground. We have been photographed, searched, and had forms filled out in various police stations, but they prefer to continue the game: "You have no identity cards, therefore no place of domicile, therefore you are vagabonds, so back to jail." We are not sent to jail, however, but are kept waiting in various headquarters without being able to sleep or eat. We pray, sing, observe silence, and try to meditate. Repeated questioning brings nothing new, and one can hardly hold people indefinitely for vagabondage. "You didn't get authorization for your demonstration; you are guilty of participating in a demonstration that was not approved." Back in jail for a few hours again, more photographs, and then on to a judge who sentences us to jail. "No identity cards, then no mail, no packages, no visits; after six months of that, maybe their ideas will have changed. . . ."

Is it necessary to agree with me before protesting against this kind of justice? Ought I to change my way of acting so that it is defensible in your eyes? You know that I am fighting loyally for what I believe to be the truth and that is why you do not refuse to defend me. Nevertheless, the purpose that we are pursuing is questionable to you, and you refuse to defend it. This concern for truth establishes a bond between us far stronger than our differences of opinion. . . .

You will not prevent me from thinking that the Incarnation is the mystery of a God who, in order to recall to us his presence in every man, refuses to have any identity other than of a man. But we go on with the game, saying, "There is no room for you in the inn," and end up saying, "If you are the Son of God, come down from the cross"—and he plays the game to the end. Of course, in the face of that divine comedy, our poor gestures of peace will never be anything more than the grimaces of buffoons.

The recent declaration of the French hierarchy has been a great joy to me. Insubordination has been clearly condemned, and this is just. I do not favor insubordination, and have been strongly criticized for condemning it; but such an attitude is one of refusal, and seems to question the very principle of law. One can regret, however, that we have been firmly reminded of the duty to disobey in cases of torture and other excesses only after these practices have been going on for five or six years. Our attitude consists of an external submission to authority, accepting the law and its sanctions; "Render to Caesar" does not ask for more. But don't we have the duty to affirm the rights of conscience? Earlier this month a bishop whose judgment you have helped me appreciate wrote me with essentially this position: "If you remain on the strictly moral level, your role will be to affirm the absolute character of morality, which is too often forgotten in our day." Neither you, nor he, nor I have ever thought that the moral level is simply one of ideas.

For those who are not satisfied with the common morality well stated by the declaration of the hierarchy, for those who are not satisfied by obedience (even with the understanding that there are exceptions), we must teach the morality of disobedience and its serious consequences. To those for whom "Law is the power of sin," we must recall that one can go beyond the law and sin only by the accomplishment of the law, not its destruction.

Don't think that everything is as simple and logical as this reasoning. Each time a young man joins us there is the question: Is he conscious of his act? Will he know how to accept all its consequences? Does he know that we can do nothing to lighten his burden, that we can only serve the same cause together? Is he deceiving himself? In the deepest part of his being, what is driving him to this position? And the response to these questions is never definitive. Why should it be for him, since it isn't for us? Are we so sure that we are not dressing up our little ideas, habits, and interests in the mantle of Truth and Justice? Are we so sure of never deviating, never collapsing? There is only one answer: "Peace on earth to men of good will."

Our efforts at a community life, our demonstrations and imprisonment—all this is precisely for the purpose of understanding the demands of this way that we have chosen, or that has chosen us. That is what is constructive. We who wish to change the world are learning how difficult it is to change one's self, and that it is there that the nonviolent revolution begins.

In contrast to Jeanson's group, the nonviolent tried to give a public witness; they refused to support violence against anyone, and asked to be assigned to some constructive work. The volunteers even opened up workyards when young men who had refused to obey the call to arms came to work on jobs that had some public utility. Each time they sent a letter to the military authorities, and then waited for the police to come—sometimes a week, sometimes several months later—to take them away to prison.

Thus, by diverse routes, some more political, others more spiritual, the witness of refusing to co-operate in repression was publicly given. A manifesto of 121 intellectuals and artists, and the trial of members of the Jeanson group helped to make this refusal to obey known to the public. Public opinion, which was beginning to tire of the prolonged war, became more willing to listen to appeals for peace. The youth groups, in which the Catholic Left played a key role, protested against atrocities and demanded negotiations. When the generals who were in command in Algiers tried to organize a military *putsch* in April 1961, it was the young and noncommissioned officers—who had been involved in these movements and unions—that organized the resistance of their units; in this effort, Catholics seemed to have been more active than Communists.

The end was now in sight. There was another difficult year: plastic bombs were thrown at the offices of leftist publications, and even at the homes of contributors; but the terrorism of the OAS only produced larger protests in which the CFTC and the Catholic students took an active part. In the spring of 1962 negotiations finally came to an end, prompting the OAS to launch their last futile attacks in the large cities of Algiers; Moslems, French liberals, Catholics, and even priests were massacred by supporters of General Salan. Finally, the government took action, and peace was established. It was a peace that Catholics had played a large part in bringing about, and for once it could be said that moral concerns had outweighed politics.

VII

World Violence
and World Peace

Is Christianity Western?

1940 to 1958 was the age of discovery. French Christians saw fully revealed the new world toward which their forefathers had set forth. They saw all the peoples of the earth gathered together in a new solidarity. They witnessed the triumph of reason; the old, rural civilizations, wrapped in contemplation of the eternal order of nature, were on the verge of obliteration. Production mattered less than consumption, work less than leisure. A good many Christians, without any reservations other than those of a believer aware of the reality of sin, took up the cause of man, not to idolize him, but to understand him, serve him, and with God's help try to save him. Seldom in the history of the Church has faith taken a more moving form—a hidden stream.

210

The struggle of French Catholics against colonialism, as we saw in the last chapter, was not simply a political fight. Its most fundamental motivation was religious. Faithfulness to God required them to encourage a genuine dialogue among all the peoples of the world, whereas colonialist attitudes had reflected the fundamental error that Christianity was merely a Western religion. In their insistence on a more genuinely catholic Christianity, one capable of embracing the rich cultures and religious traditions of non-Western areas, the pioneering experiment of Father Jules Monchanin was increasingly invoked as a symbolic example. Monchanin, after many years as a priest in France, left at the age of forty-four to serve under an Indian bishop, and devoted the remainder of his life to contemplation, founding an ashrama and emphasizing the connection between Indian and traditional Christian spirituality. In an analogous spirit, Robert de Montvalon called for a greater understanding of the aspirations of the "new nations" of Asia and Africa:

Let us try to put ourselves in the place of an African or an Asian aspiring toward independence in a country under white domination, where Christians are only a small minority led by bishops and priests who themselves are almost all white men, and who have not reached the kind of maturity needed to be true representatives of Christianity. How could that African or Asian help misunderstanding the supranational nature of the Church? Doctrinal affirmations, however just and necessary they may be, will not convince such a man that he is wrong. He is waiting for Christians to give overwhelming witness to the catholicity of the Church. . . .

However paradoxical, however painful it may be, the Christendom which sent out missionaries has become a sign of contradiction, and perhaps a cause of scandal, since its members are also citizens of the colonial powers. We might have wished it otherwise. We may have envisioned a Church established "firmly and forever" amidst the people of the overseas territories before the question of independence was raised. But this was not what happened. It is therefore essential that European Christians demonstrate unequivocally their desire to help the autochthonous churches to reach full maturity; they must, in other words, demonstrate that the Church is catholic. And since the witness of a Christian is not judged valid unless it also encompasses concrete realities—just as a man cannot seriously believe in heaven unless his feet are firmly set on earth —French Christians must be the first to show that they understand the political, economic, and social problems of overseas peoples, and that, without hypocrisy, they want to help solve these problems. . . .

The present crisis of the underdeveloped continents is full of dangers, but Christians have an obligation to make it an opportunity for Christianity to expand into new areas. In the past, history provided Christian expansion with a limited and equivocal tool: colonization. The present crisis of the former colonies, which is no less than the renaissance of these peoples, may well figure as a new instrument which Christian intelligence should not fail to put to good use.

The stakes are high. What will the Church be like in a hundred years if white Christians' possessiveness prevents it from keeping pace with the development of the new nations, a growth which it foresaw? The terrible poverty of these nations defines the basic economic task of the next fifty years, by which both Communism and capitalism will be judged. The ashes of European nationalisms are not yet cold: we run the risk of replacing them with racism on a continental scale. Already the image of war as an adventure is coming back into style: "Enlist and see the world." The cult of the hereditary enemy is ready to set up a new idol.

We must accept the demise of colonialism in order to bring about a rebirth: to believe that we could accomplish such a thing without effort would be childish; perhaps only defeat is in store for us. But as Europeans we would find it easier to overcome our prejudices if we were not all the victims of badly misunderstood traditions. . . .

In the past the white man, with his weapons and his traders, thought he had united the nations. The truth was that he dominated them; he was the master; he alone stood in the center of his colonial expositions amidst continents under orders to echo his words back to him. Today voices are being raised on every side. Conversation between peoples is being resumed.[1]

When the French bishops of West Africa and Togo published a long declaration on current problems in 1955, the text read:

In the sphere of politics, you aspire to autonomy, to be able to manage your own affairs. This aspiration is legitimate. Every people, every society endowed with an original personality, has in effect the right to affirm and develop that personality, in order to contribute a new dimension to the human community. We desire to see a sincere and brotherly dialogue treating these questions [of seeking independence] based on the equality of all men and all races, and on respect for differences, which are an enrichment when they complement each other instead of struggling against one another. . . .

The Church is above all universal. . . . And it is because

of that universality that it transcends every border line and
ultimately can bring its message to individual men in every
country and in every era, adapting itself to them as they
are, without ceasing to unite them to God and to the rest of
the world. The Church is a meeting place.[2]

Of course, the game is not won. No one imagines that
the gates of earthly paradise are about to reopen. But,
when legislators and other leaders from Madagascar were
imprisoned for political reasons, an amnesty committee
was formed by Christians, headed by Louis Massignon.
When the Algerian War was at its height, French Catholics, following the example of Archbishop Duval of Algiers,
refused categorically to consider it a religious war between
Christianity and Islam. The Comité chrétien pour l'entente
France-Islam, led by Louis Massignon and André de Per-
etti, appealed to Christians to turn away from war toward
the brotherhood of all believers.

But no one was under the illusion that simply announcing religious ecumenism and political solidarity would
bring them about. They had to be built brick by brick.

The condition we now refer to as "underdevelopment"
—obviously a white man's word—attracts more and more
attention, thanks to the work of sociologists and econo-
mists such as Father Lebret and François Perroux, the Pax
Christi movement, the work of Catholic journalists, and
many others. Lebret, the Dominican priest who founded
Economie et Humanisme, traveled constantly from one
continent to another, insisting that the obligation of the
rich to help the poor meant that the West must give up its
proprietary attitude.

The greatest tragedy in the world is not the poverty of

the "have-nots," but the lack of awareness of the "haves."

The awareness of the have-nots is at last fully awakened; the era of passivity of the masses is on its way out. Increasing literacy, access to newspapers and radio, and the ostentation both of the upper classes of autochthonous populations and of foreigners brings home to the dispossessed the realization that there exists a fraction of mankind which has too much. Henceforth, resignation is impossible. Everywhere a reaction against passivity has set in, taking widely varied forms. But given the fact that the West still insists on possessing certain comforts, and is intent on accumulating more and more wealth, this reaction turns principally against Westerners. The whole world is feverish with nationalist outbursts by subject peoples. The colonial territories started this reaction, and then it spread to independent countries which felt their sovereignty indirectly threatened, not only by economic power, but also by all kinds of programs which were not disinterested.

The privileged social classes of those caught up in this movement (feudal lords, landowners, newly rich capitalists, middle-class people whose wealth is based on commerce, administrators, military officers, civil servants) have realized that by influencing these movements of unrest to evolve toward nationalism, they can protect, at least temporarily, their positions or their ambitions.

Thus, bit by bit, the West is being put to shame. The underequipped world is forming a united front against it. Their amorphous discontent, turned against the West, becomes a clearly directed aggression. China, emancipated from Western influence, takes on the appearance of a model of progress, the imitation of which can guarantee access to prosperity.

The unfortunate thing is that the West does not wish to understand this, does not seem able to grasp it. It is imprisoned in its outmoded concepts, whether they be straight-forwardly colonialist, or simply involve loyalty to a doctrine and an economic system which are outdated in relation to the needs and aspirations of the poorer nations. . . .

Bound to the outlook of a narrow economy based on profit, it does not see the demands of a universal economy of need, which its rival, the Communism that is dominant, upholds at least in principle. Defending ourselves against Communism has become an obsession, but we fail to realize that Communism cannot be defeated by force, but only by the "reconversion" of economic power and of Western culture to the service of all mankind. We think in terms of military alliances and strategic provisions—that is, in terms of being served by others. . . .

Now that the time has come to stand apart from short-term involvements, and to take hold of the world's evolution and turn it toward middle-range and long-range goals, the West is trying to patch up the breakdowns in worn-out machinery on a day-to-day basis. But it is no longer the creator of civilization; the advent of a new type of civilization has become imperative, one which must be universal, whose principles were outlined in the International Declaration of the Rights of Man. When every effort should be focused on giving people the means to put these rights into practice, the West is haggling over the elaboration of inadequate aid programs. It gives assistance to poor countries, explaining to the more privileged sectors of the population that this is for their own interest or prestige.

But if the West really cared about their interest and prestige, a different attitude would be required. To the person from an underdeveloped country, the sophisticated white man, despite the beginnings of disinterestedness which he sometimes shows, is one who wants in one way or another to "take others in," to "put something over on them," to secure raw materials, military bases, markets. From this point of view, North American political speeches are as antipolitical as possible. Their aid programs are based on greed or fear, not on justice and love. Then they are astonished that all they receive in return is mistrust, aggression, and hate.

The West is committing suicide by closing itself in. . . . Basically, the problem is one of a reversal of values, leading to a new framework for judging the world, and to new modes of relationships between peoples, including Communist peoples.

By letting Communism have a monopoly on the complete defense and advancement of man, the West is letting the world sink into nostalgia for an illusory humanism; furthermore it is shirking its elementary obligations toward the peoples already dominated by Communism.

The tragedy is that the West has abandoned the scale of values which might be able to create a new civilization.

In this scale of values, a person is judged on his own merits, for his actual and potential value. Thus there can be no question of enslaving him, on one pretext or another; he must be helped to become a free person, free from poverty and able to choose his own goals. The West, which claims to be a great champion of freedom, still wants to make freedom dependent on choosing an economic system which misuses it. . . .

We always end up uncovering the special interests of individuals, of groups, or of peoples, without any concern for the universal good. . . .[3]

Blessed Are the Peacemakers

Recourse to violence is still widespread. The use of torture and the dropping of the atomic bomb are the most obvious examples. The late Archbishop Chappoulie proved his clearsightedness on this subject in an address in 1955, when French emotions were aroused by the Algerian War:

One would have to be blind to the degree of violence which racial conflict can reach, and to the bloody dramas it provokes—from lynchings and massacres to terrorist and counterterrorist attacks—and blind to the deep and tenacious rancors they leave behind, not to realize that in this area the Church can be a powerful force for calm, conciliation, and, ultimately, for unity among men.

We French are especially able to understand this because we are close to the terrible problems caused by racial conflict. Christians cannot allow North Africans, Negroes, natives of Madagascar, to be treated as second-class men and objects for exploitation.

They have a right to justice, which should not provide less protection to an accused man because he was born an Arab or because he has dark skin. He is a son of God like everyone else, and deserves to be valued as highly. Furthermore, Christians cannot subscribe to forms of mass repression which hold cheap the individual life of a native, deny him the right to defend himself before sentence is passed, and sentence him to death without a trial, as if he were a dangerous animal that must be prevented from doing harm. Those who make criminal attacks on European lives and property must be disciplined and public order restored, but for Christians this does not justify the collective murder of the whole population of a village, or those "round-ups" in which innocent and guilty alike are arrested, on the grounds that both are of the same race, and that the summary execution of people of an inferior race is not a crime. I am not speaking out of passion when I say this, but simply repeating the traditional teaching of the Church: " 'The mass shooting of innocent people as a reprisal for the crime of one individual is not an act of justice, but sanctioned injustice. To shoot innocent hostages does not become a right simply because it has been made a necessity of war.' "*4

Father Régamey goes further: Since the use of torture and the atomic bomb are not the only manifestations of the violence which lies at the heart of the modern world, non-violence "poses a question which the Christian conscience cannot elude." Hoping against hope, he seeks a path founded on stark, lucid analysis, tracing the sources of violence to the corruption of the aggressive drives, to rejected love, and finally to lack of discrimination on the part of the intelligence:

We think correctly as long as we keep alive in us, as we judge and reason, a sense of the living and rich reality out of which we are constructing our own conceptual patterns.** We are, alas, constantly in danger of reducing reality to the ideas we have about it, and we then proceed to falsify the ideas themselves. We are constantly careless in giving serious thought to what we say; our reflection is constantly defective. We seek escape in words which run away with us. How rarely one comes across real thinking, in which intelligence is truly present. And how often we lose the meaning of what we once saw clearly. So we patch up, we build systems, "a theory out of bits of ignorance," as Stendhal put it. If we look closely, what often passes for thought is most frequently a gap covered up by a lot of pretences.

Now it is generally the emotions that suggest these pre-

---

* Pius XII Address to the Members of the IV International Congress of Criminal Law, October 3, 1953, Documentation catholique 1/11/1953, col. 351–2, 353.

** This requires a continual return to the sense-impression (conversio ad phantasmata), Sum. Theol., Ia Pars, qu. 84, art. 7.

tences. The dulling of perception and the loss of control of
the mind over itself leaves a vacuum which is filled by
instinctual urges. As one no longer has any serious grasp of
what one is talking about, one accommodates the truth and
gives the emotions free rein in conversation. They then
take control of behavior.

This evil is made worse by the appalling increase of
modern images and superficial slogans. Everything around
us conspires to dissipate our minds in half-truths. Not so
long ago, the majority of men knew very few things, but
they were all real, objectively as well as subjectively; men
had an immediate and comprehensive experience of what
they knew; their knowledge had come at first hand; they
assimilated it and quite naturally adapted their behavior to
it. Thus they were wise in their knowledge; it had a spiritual quality. They "kept things in their hearts." Moral
awareness went hand in hand with knowledge. Our mind,
by contrast, is just like a sheet of paper that retains only the
news of the last fortnight, to use an image of Charles Péguy.
A flood of information which has not been assimilated by
personal thinking does violence to the mind, by stupefying
and blinding it. It has no longer any certainty to speak of; it
makes an arbitrary choice among various opinions. A
Marxist naturally says: "When one has accepted the
primacy of economic development, psychological and spiritual explanations of the world just fade away." This acceptance produces results, but it ruthlessly cuts out a whole
area of life.

Let us be watchful, or everything will fall into the mould
of "organization man" who is so typical of the modern
world. Everything, even religion, is reduced to dry for-
mulae, to what can be explained and docketed. Everything
suffers violence and does violence to the real, often beginning with any true spirit who cherishes "nonviolence."

Anyone who is in the slightest degree acquainted with pacifist literature will have read passages like this one: "We recognize no human authority. We only accept one king and ruler (God, conscience or what have you). We love every country as much as our own. A nation has no right to defend itself against its enemies." Abstractions like this do great harm to essential and vital realities.

Meanwhile, qualified specialists, technicians, technocrats, using rigorous methods, arrive at conclusions which are perfectly objective within their own frameworks; but they reduce reality to the measurable. There can, of course, be no objection to measuring the measurable. Needless to say, man, being subject to time and space, to the "elements of this world" and all they involve, is the subject-matter of the statistician, chemist, physicist and economist. . . . Their work is, of course, necessary. Equally, of course, economic, social and political techniques are going to benefit greatly from it. But then, as one thing leads to another, with astonishing speed and on a huge scale, the combination of these technical means turns into an autonomous universe, developing along its own lines, and substituting itself for nature and man.

The primitive techniques were simply "intermediaries between man and his environment,"* through which man could exercise some mastery over that environment. In this way he worked for particular ends, and used only such means as were required for life and to adorn it.** Today he has lost his mastery over his techniques, they no longer provide him with any goal or purpose, he can no longer tell why he strives for progress along all the lines of possible development. It has become a combination of factors

* J. Ellul, La technique, ou l'enjeu du siècle (Paris: A. Colin, 1954), p. 58.
** Ibid., pp. 60 ff.

which of themselves bring forth further results. *Discoveries
and inventions thus indefinitely give rise to one another.
Man has become the slave of a process which unfolds itself
as a deterministic system governed by sheer efficiency, but
with no end in view.** Within this metaphysical misuse lies
a radical and essential violence which results ineluctably in
indefinite chains of violence. When one examines the pro-
cesses which led up to the dropping of the first atomic
bomb on Hiroshima, one sees men being led step by step,
so that one cannot decide the precise moment when one of
those responsible for it made a decisive act, or even who
was responsible. Men have been caught out at their own
game and have alienated themselves. "They are all being
driven by external forces to an external end: the object to
be attained, the movement toward it."** Where does it
lead to? When must one make a stand? How can one withdraw? This is the crux; the setting in motion of certain
causes inevitably begetting others sometimes leads so
clearly to such excesses that modern man must prepare
himself at some point to make this stand, just as the martyrs
of the early centuries had to be prepared for martyrdom.
There must be downright refusals, no more talk. One has to
oppose evil, even if one cannot prevent it; the time will
come when one will have to choose to be a victim rather
than an accomplice. This preparation entails taking care
that our consciences do not, meanwhile, become blunted.
We cannot hope to build an ark which will sail through the
waters of perdition. There is more than a mere atmosphere
that needs rejection in our technical world. But let us not
take refuge in a foolish optimism which can only be a form
of voluntary blindness. We need to be constantly on our

---

* *Ibid.*, pp. 90–91. All technical progress has an end, but it is simply
an immediate one with no ultimate end in view such as is worthy of man.
  ** *Ibid.*, p. 389.

guard against the seductive illusion that a distinction can be made between our techniques and the use we make of them; indulging in such daydreams as "that man will direct his discoveries in the service of good and not of evil . . . that he will produce health-giving drugs and not lethal gases, atomic energy and no more atomic bombs, commercial airliners instead of fighter planes," etc.*

There is not much that man can now direct. What we must face boldly is this almost indivisible combination of the features of modern technology which powerfully limits the possibility of reorientation, and which Ellul describes as "automation of technical choice, auto-accretion, indivisibility," this latter term signifying that one cannot accept certain techniques and reject others for moral reasons, for instance: they are all necessary to each other, "a linking up of techniques, a universalism." Let us face it: it means the progressive extension of this process over the whole world so that it includes all human activities, even those of the mind—in short "autonomy" covering economics and politics, social conditions and morality.**

"Only a technical power can stand up to another technical power: the rest has been thrown overboard." They oppose one another in the same manner as the blind forces of nature. As Malraux puts it, we are faced with "a re-awakening of blind fate." The "thinking reed" has always been the plaything of storms. But it is he himself who has unleashed these. He recognizes in them, on a vastly magnified scale, the results of his own pretensions at spiritual mastery, while so much of his spiritual potentiality escapes him. The worst thing about it is that these blind forces are not merely content with enslaving and crushing him in their mad destructive progress, they require his collabora-

* Ibid., pp. 89–90 (with some reservations however).
** Ibid., pp. 75–134.

tion; they exert their influence even upon the conditions of
his inner freedom (through psychological techniques), and
the time may come when he will no longer be able to see
his way to exercise any free activity within it.[5]

These denunciations were not written out of hatred for
the modern world or in the hope of inspiring the kind of
pacifism which is based on weakness. Recognizing that
there are no easy solutions, Emmanuel Mounier criticized
the ambiguities of pacifism in these terms:

It might be asked how so many convinced pacifists were
able during the German Occupation to become the leading
collaborators of a regime whose principle was war. That
this phenomenon was repeated in all of occupied Europe,
under the most diverse conditions, leaves us with the conjec-
ture that it was in some way linked to their previous attitude, and led them on the same path. If they had refused to
participate in the Resistance in order to avoid taking part
in violence, they would have been within the logic of their
pacifism. But why did they cheerfully, and sometimes
avidly, take sides with force? The only explanation would
seem to be an inner defenselessness, resulting from indifference to any other value than a diseased, an almost obscene,
will to live, which is as foreign to the power of life as
eroticism is to the power of love.
Such an intellectual and emotional inversion of forceful
affirmation was often an abdication of responsibility, and
became an asexual passion for servility, a secret consent to
the strength of the conqueror. Even those imbued with the
noblest feelings did not realize that by constantly fixing
them on the rejection of feeling, they were sometimes
encouraging a desperate and feminine desire for force.
By wanting to remain among the living without examin-

ing the content of life, they emptied life of its very meaning. Living means probing, re-examining, creating; for
them, it meant enduring, being left in peace. Modern wars
always raise the question of revolution. There is a kind of
pacifism which fails to distinguish between protest against
war and a general protest against injustice. This pacifism
objects more to the upheaval war entails than to the scandal of the means it employs. For this kind of pacifist, peace
means "let me alone". . . .

The weakness common to all these attitudes is evident in
the way men demand peace today. They do not will to have
peace; they simply wait for it; they have let themselves be
persuaded that everything is beyond their power, that un-
fathomable combinations and inexorable destinies determine war and peace, that peace will be accorded or war
unleashed, and they will not bear the slightest responsibility
for it. A man like Garry Davis* attacks this kind of fatal-
ism head on, and demonstrates plainly that a simple human
gesture can disconcert the higher powers, and that thousands of similar bold acts would paralyze them. But people
do not take this example to heart and run a risk themselves;
they look on, applaud, and ask for his autograph. But unless there is some impact on their actions, a "peace rally"
may also be a great demonstration of collective cowardice.
Peace is not something to edify the passive listener but
something to engage man's hands and heart.[6]

The spirit of peace should inspire both prophetic upheavals and humble undertakings. "Resistance to evil of
necessity becomes subject to human realities," Father Régamey reminded us. "We must constantly re-examine solutions which are still impure. But except in extreme cases,

* An American citizen who caused a stir in 1947–1950 by declaring himself a citizen of the world.

these will usually be neither simple rejection of violence nor returning evil for evil. . . . We have entered upon an era in which we are likely to witness a multiplication of situations comparable to those which the Christians of the first century could solve only by living in constant danger, or even by martyrdom. . . . Discernment must be exercised on three fronts: theology, depth psychology, and politics."[7]

The Brotherhood of Man

To anyone working for human brotherhood, the strength of routine, group pride, and simple apathy leaves no room for illusions. Of course, the wide response which greeted the encyclical *Pacem in Terris* gave hope to many French Catholics. The colonial crisis had led some of them to rediscover the theology of Las Casas and Vitoria, who had drawn up a basic outline for a code of international law and a world ethics at the dawn of modern times, to give some order to the beginnings of colonialism. For four centuries Christians had made a mockery of this theology, but Pope John had given it a new resonance.

At this juncture of their history, French Christians find themselves faced with the task of deciphering the meaning of a planet that has shrunk and is glutted with knowledge. They are not the only ones facing this problem, to be sure. The stakes are enormous: all humanity, all Christianity are involved. The Christian learns from Christ that all men are brothers and are called upon to unite. But he cannot limit himself to preaching an ideal of union or announcing the perfect unity in another world. He must try to make it a reality today, using the materials which history provides, and this is a political task. Its accomplishment means that all men must be gathered together—not in the visible Church but in working toward this goal. Christians are contributing to remaking man in God's image. Christ illuminates history, and history strives to perfect the work of Christ, who alone can redeem it.

Neither the paths nor the goals are clear, but, as Jean Frisque wrote, the gathering of the peoples of the world is a question God puts to us, and which we ask of him:

> The Church's mission is to gather the dispersed children of God into the family of the Father. This gathering, which will be manifested only in the world beyond death, is the work of the Holy Spirit in conjunction with the adopted children of the Father united to the incarnate Word.

> Does that mean that every human project of world brotherhood here on earth is doomed to failure, or is meaningless? Not at all. On the contrary, it makes this effort more necessary than ever, and Christians have a special reason to collaborate in it.

> In fact, while the "filial assent" of the child of God is the only thing that can build the Kingdom of God, it is nonetheless true that the substance of this assent is the consent of obedience unto death. And although the creaturely task inspired by this kind of obedience is not in itself a way to salvation, it nevertheless constitutes for all time the necessary support for the filial assent upon which the Kingdom is built.

> In what does the creature's task in the building of genuine catholicity take form in this world, if not in working for brotherhood and peace—in promoting unity through diversity? Of course, this cannot be just another human plan; it must be inspired by Christian love which excludes no one and which recognizes the same basic dignity in every man.

> We realize that this evangelical scheme of world brotherhood will never be fully realized in this world; sin contin-

ues to obstruct the advance of humanity in its quest for
unity. But to abandon this task would mean abandoning
the Church's effort at universality.

If our view of history is accurate, the task of the Church
today is to become part of the extraordinarily complex spiritual dynamism that propels the history of those cultures
in which the mystery of Christ is not yet rooted. In this
effort to be present, the Church's mandate is to show that
Christ is the unhoped-for fulfillment of the deepest desires
animating this spiritual dynamism.

Jesus Christ, the only Savior of the world, will be made
manifest in the heart of a mystery of tradition: In the trans-
mission of the mystery of Christ from the cultural universe
of the white man to other cultural universes, the true face
of the one mediator will be revealed in its essence, thus
accomplishing man's destiny in the paschal victory over the
walls of separation. . . .

The evangelization of the modern world is at stake in the
great debate between cultures which is taking place before
our very eyes. We are as yet only at the preliminary stages
of this debate, but we know already that inevitably man's
truth is dramatically involved, because the extension of scientific and technical civilization brings men into closer and
closer contact with each other. On the level of the geo-
graphico-cultural universes into which mankind is divided,
the walls of separation have an exceptional density, and
force is taking the place of dialogue.

The fact that the Church is concretely bound to the cultural sphere of the white man is an evil only insofar as the
Church itself clings to this bond. If, on the contrary, the
Church takes its stand at the crossroads of cultures, with
the awareness that this is its most pressing duty, and that
twenty centuries of history have prepared it to play this role
correctly, then it will be truly the light of the world, be-

cause it will have reached the very heart of the human
adventure. . . .[8]

Paul André Lesort has described how every man is
called upon to participate in this adventure:

We should ask each other what significance the simple
but fundamental realities have for us—birth and death,
suffering, happiness, love, evil. Then we might ask what
meaning men have for each other. . . .
Let us arrive at an understanding of how each of us
conceives man's situation in the world, his development,
and that of the world; of man's freedom, and of the requirements for what we will call, in a general way, salvation. And in these personal relationships with the world, let
us identify the links and the breaks: community and solitude, obedience and freedom, love and renunciation, action and contemplation, our personal relationship with the
Absolute. What do I call the Absolute? Do I contemplate
it? Do I speak to it? In what way? And how can I approach
it? On the basis of these soundings, from the replies which
in all likelihood are stumbling and inarticulate, men can
proceed to ask themselves once again how they read the
signs surrounding them—not only what the signs reveal and
what they tell, but what they hide, what they cannot tell,
because it is inexpressible, and because the inexpressible is
perhaps the ineffable.
We can then perhaps learn, or at least sense, what is
beyond signs in other men's universes. And this would also
be learning—or, at least sensing—the same thing about the
total universe which our faith ought to encompass. For
each of us this would mean a rediscovery both of the extent
and the limits of the visible universe. It would mean learning to make the transition from the visible to the invisible;

to recognize—though through a glass darkly—the presence of the wholly Other. This recognition leads immediately to the recognition of mystery, since in order to follow this common path of mutual questioning about fundamentals, we have to accept the mystery of the relationship of each man with the wholly Other. For each person who consents to undertake this encounter, it means both detaching his own belief from the historical matrix, and discovering the relationship of the entire person, through the medium of his history and culture, with all that transcends him.[9]

This is the direction in which French Catholics are moving. Even before the last war, Mounier had said: "History makes us somewhat modest. Politics will find only a small place in it. The great upheavals of civilization, which alone leave a lasting mark, proceed at a different pace and with a different kind of perseverance. We should be less proud, and less impatient. We have barely begun our job."

Conclusion
A New Christianity

IF someone were to ask what has changed the most in France in the past twenty years, we would answer: the Catholic Church. When the war began, the French Church still viewed itself as a fortress besieged by secularism, modernism, and Communism. Its dominant tradition was bound to rural structures, to thousands of parishes of which the great majority date from the twelfth century; democracy was still held suspect; civic duty consisted in loving the fatherland with an exclusive passion; religious duty meant going to church regularly; moral duty meant steering clear of "worldly" temptations. The Church of France, rooted in one of the strongest peasantries in the world, hardened by the attacks of revolutionaries and Socialists, priding itself on an extraordinary number of saints and theologians, still clung to the notion of Christendom as an alliance of the land, the parish priest, and conservative political power. The foundations of that Christendom were being constantly eroded; another world was already being built,

231

whose values and customs seemed far from those of the Church. Even before the war, a few avant-garde Christians saw what was happening: theologians like De Lubac and Chenu; journals like *Sept, Temps présent, La vie intellectuelle,* and *Esprit* had begun the fight against the Church's identification with the established order. At the same time, sometimes influenced by these thinkers, Catholic Action movements aroused new fervor among Christian youth. People started to read the Bible again, and simply to meditate on the Gospel. They rediscovered the fact that Christ, born into a worker's family, had preached love for the poor and not love of property. They began to see in the hopes of revolutionaries the reflection of a Christian hope that had been disappointed.

As we have seen, the shock of the German Occupation crystallized these attitudes. Many young Christians, obliged to rely on their consciences, and sometimes even to challenge the directives of certain bishops, discovered the eternally new face of the Gospel teachings, and threw themselves wholeheartedly into the Liberation movement which, after freeing their land and institutions, was also to be a liberation of souls. Undoubtedly, such a situation gave rise to illusions, and even to certain pretensions; that was the unavoidable price for the movement of renewal to which the French Church owed its new aspect, and which might even have drawn the whole Church into its orbit in a reform without heresy if the circumstances, both inside the Church and outside it, had been propitious.

But before long, admonitions and condemnations began to fall upon the pioneers. From 1949 to 1959, there was hardly an initiative, whether theological, liturgical, or pastoral, which was not attacked. Some imprudences had been committed, to be sure; this book does not try to conceal the excesses caused by theorists who were too enthusiastic or too much influenced by the dominant ideological currents

—particularly Marxism. Nevertheless, it is hypocritical to weigh the excesses against the achievements and condemn the good in the name of the bad, since there is no such thing in human history as an achievement which has not been paid for by some mistakes, and the Church, too, is a human institution. As we review that era, which was both inspiring and painful, we are struck by one thing: in the final analysis there were very few apostasies, and no schisms. It is true that several priest-workers renounced their priesthood; a small number of laymen became Communists. But what is that compared to the astonishing revival of vitality which touched every sector of our Church, and to the wonderful surprise of the Council, whose groundwork was laid by these searchings and experiments, dangerous as they sometimes may have been? One cannot read these texts written by avant-garde Catholics without realizing that the bold steps made by the Council were foreshadowed by them, beginning with the preamble upon which John XXIII was to insist: the confession of the Church's blind spots, which had lasted too long, and the desire to become humble of heart in order to know and love better the men and the ideas which remain outside the Church. Avant-garde Catholics took the first risks which made *aggiornamento* possible. They do not claim any privileges or thanks for it—they simply hope that others will draw a lesson from their experience.

Breaking with the old-style conception of a fortress Church was the prerequisite for setting out on the missionary adventure spearheaded by the priest-workers, of which they remained the symbol. But, as we have tried to show, one could not, like the social Catholics of the nineteenth century, go to the workers offering a "social doctrine" of justice and charity. Something further was required of the new missionaries: they themselves had to change, and try to change the Church, so that they could change others.

Confronted with a modern world which had grown up outside of Christianity, Christians gave up excommunicating
others, or scorning them, and began trying to understand
and love them. They wanted to remake themselves into
men like the rest, to restrict themselves to the bare essentials, and go armed only with the light, the truth, and the
hope of their faith. Thus they returned to St. Paul's asceticism; the Christian will become different from the rest of
men only if at the start he resembles them; he will be close
to God only if he has first lived with men. The working-
class world was the ideal place to practice this renunciation
and make this effort. It is still too soon to draw up the
balance sheet of the priest-worker experience. On the surface, there are few positive results: most of the priest-
workers had to abandon their efforts. And yet, at the
Council, bishops from Asia and Latin America asked to
have this experiment reinstated and adapted to present-day
circumstances. This was because the witness given in the
working-class suburbs of Paris represented much more
than an "experiment" with certain original features: it was
the beginning of a reconciliation between the Church and
the poor, and by the same token a plea that the Church
modify its attitude, its customs, and its liturgy, so that it
would be capable of striking new roots. It was the birth of a
new concept of the sacred, no longer based on rural civilization and monarchical society, which had inspired previous forms of the visible Church—its hierarchy, its ceremonies, its language, and too often its behavior—but
founded on industrial civilization and democratic society.

The consequences of such an enterprise are incalculable;
they go far beyond the problem it was designed to solve.
French Catholics are now noticing that over the last ten
years the working class has lost its special character. Workers no longer live on the outskirts of cities as they used to,

and many of them are no longer poor. Although a fraction of the working class still exists as a separate proletariat, another sector is drawing closer to the class of technicians, and is beginning to share in the general culture, at least through the channels of mass media. But on two basic fronts the barrier which the priest-workers were trying to break down is still standing: in the first place, the world of technology continues to live its autonomous life, outside of Christian values. Even when it does not express its hope and its Promethean will through Marxism, it remains consciously, often proudly atheist. Of course it sometimes makes room for religion, or even turns to it for aid. But we cannot say that the Church, in spite of the remarkable prestige of Teilhard de Chardin, has yet dared to undertake a confrontation in depth with a society which, having gained mastery over certain natural forces, is now trying to control its own future. How, and on what level, will the encounter be possible? Simply "adapting" the Church or modernizing it is no answer. It is all very well for the Church to use automobiles and television, but that is not enough. Sometimes we are afraid that the Church will stop there, that it will be satisfied with the place allotted it by a society which, not feeling really threatened, tolerates it with good grace. The "naturalization" desired by Cardinal Suhard and sought by the priest-workers was the very opposite of this complacent modernization which is sometimes presented as a bold move. The modern world is quite capable of assimilating religion along with the rest, of turning it into a spectacle, a status symbol, or a psychotherapy. But the worker-missionaries were seeking to make contact at a deeper level: the stratum on which a new city is founded, beyond material satisfactions, in the struggle for justice and personal dignity. These goals have been temporarily obscured by the acquisition of comforts, but they

are not dead, and they will rise up again with increased
vigor: the tyranny of profit and consumption does not fulfill man's needs. Vast masses of people are still spiritually
proletarian. Behind the veil of nihilism, one can feel the
stirring of a great need for significance. Without a substan-
tial renewal, will the Church be able to answer this need?

Furthermore, while poverty is diminishing in Western
Europe, it nonetheless is in the ascendancy—and with increasing harshness—in half the world. We can no longer,
in all fairness, accuse the Church of being the ally of landowners and capitalists; and yet does that mean that it has
become once again the Church of the poor? Unfortunately
not. While in the industrialized countries the line between
the bourgeoisie and the working class is becoming blurred,
the breach between the industrialized and the underdeveloped countries is constantly widening. And Christianity
seems to be linked to the former rather than to the latter.
Despite all the efforts made in the past twenty years to
assist the countries emerging from colonialism, the separation between the two worlds is growing more and more
pronounced. This defines the urgent need for the conversion which the priest-workers, without success, called on
the Church to effect: the conversion to poverty, which in
the interim has eluded us even further, since the consumers'
society has succeeded not only in absorbing it but even in
discrediting it.

Renewing the bond between the Church and the poor
implies more than making a number of reforms within the
Church; it demands that laymen participate through their
action in the temporal world. The hardest scandal to bear is
that centuries of evangelization and Christian life have not
more profoundly changed social structures and economic
relationships. To be sure, Christ did not come to bring
socialism into the world. But what is the value of a faith

which does not change anything in the here-and-now? Before becoming a Marxist notion, praxis was a requirement of Christianity. The Sermon on the Mount is first and foremost a collection of practical regulations: we must feed, clothe, and house others. We will not be true to the spirit of poverty if we do not manage to put an end to a system under which part of the world grows rich while the rest goes hungry. There is no social ethic which does not ultimately lead to political action in the broadest sense of the word. The French innovators understood this, to their credit. We can be proud that so many of our Christian compatriots aligned themselves with the poor and the oppressed in this many-faceted, endless struggle.

But in this area, too, there are still problems, and solutions remain far off. Twenty-five years ago, Christians faced well-defined choices; at that time it seemed possible to change the order of things and to create a new society. For a young Catholic, joining the Resistance was a commitment which was both clear and total. But causes soon lost that beautiful simplicity. After a while no party seemed to be above reproach. And above all, the economic and social machine took on a sort of autonomy: it continued on its way oblivious of human passion and human will. It is true that the war in Algeria provided an occasion for spiritual commitment and, as we have seen, the most active French Catholics responded to it. But today, in a calmer political atmosphere, how is one to take sides? It sometimes seems as though the society which is being formed has its own rationale; as though our economy had turned on the automatic pilot; by minute touches, the technocrats program the machine in the necessary direction. Its weight and complexity are such that no party imagines that this machine could be replaced by another. Then how shall we frame those words of justice, those hopes for freedom, that need for a society of brothers which inspires avant-garde Catholics? And even beyond political options, one sometimes wonders how the Gospel can be lived in a world which is so narrowly conditioned. The young man who starts off on a career demanding something new soon has to settle down, become a cog in the wheel of some big company, and earn enough money—more and more is required—to keep his position. It is not enough to formulate principles: they have to be translated into action. And we have to face the fact that this commitment is becoming more and more difficult.

And yet a great many French Catholics manage to do it in one way or another. In this collection of texts we have given priority to ideals and positions. We would like to add a detailed report from the frontier of this new Christianity. For, in all the exposed sectors, in all the difficult undertakings, one now encounters Catholics. This is of course partly due to an ancient tradition of charity, but it is more than that, for these men and women are involved in social experiments and the creation of new institutions: everywhere —whether with older people, or with sick children, with workers' communities, agricultural co-operatives, or youth clubs—one finds Catholics involved in pilot projects. A large part of the French countryside has been reclaimed by young people trained in Catholic Action teams. Former members of the Scout movement, assembled in the group called *La Vie Nouvelle*, have founded a civic movement which advocates political commitment and community action. There would be no end to this chain, which is like a new catacomb, forming the richest spiritual and moral reserve of our people. In the indifferent mass of urban society, it seems as though a new Christianity is coming to birth. In condemning the old-style Christendom, the pioneers know that the faith our century needs must rest on communities capable of rediscovering the sources of evangelical inspiration; it should be open to contemporary life. The parish has not yet become a center of life, as the innovators hoped it would, but it has changed a great deal. More and more parishes are beginning to catch the new spirit. Prayer is different in them; so is preaching. The plaster decorations and sentimental statues have disappeared, and bare stone, rough-hewn images, floods of light, have taken their place. The Council finally ratified the diverse attempts made on every side: a rejuvenated liturgy confirms the whole movement of renewal.

But a change in the formulas, a change in the institutions, is worthless unless men change as well. "You don't look much like men reborn," Nietzsche taunted the pious Christians of his time. Today one can no longer confuse the Church with a flock of bigots and choirboys at the beck and call of a feudal hierarchy. There stand men, young people, married couples, with the full weight of their family, professional, and civic responsibilities: "The faithful," unafraid to face the world, and if necessary to speak their minds to their parish priests, or even to their bishops.

Furthermore, it is no longer possible to identify the Church with rightist politics. That is one of the factors which permits Catholics to play such a constructive role in public affairs. In cultural, political, and trade-union circles, they have no feelings of inferiority. One after another, barriers are falling. The Christian trade union has even given up its label of "Christian," and now calls itself "democratic": and, indeed, at the level of commitment to unionism, why shouldn't Catholics march shoulder to shoulder with non-Catholic workers? If the faithful have strong spiritual lives, and if they are one with the Church, then they are that much freer to become deeply involved and to be the animating spirit at the heart of the masses.

There is no guarantee that all the bishops of France have as yet realized the extent of this transformation, although some of them have set the example. We shall not soon forget the attitude of Archbishop Duval of Algiers, who today has become an Algerian; wherever a conflict breaks out, it is very rare that the local bishop does not raise his voice for justice and charity. But certain authoritarian habits are difficult to break, and the traditionalists put a kind of pressure on the bishops which is close to using threats of schism as a form of blackmail. Therefore, there are—and there will continue to be—hesitations and restraints. But one thing has been accomplished: A certain form of submissiveness which had nothing in common with Christian obedience has been banished from our Church. Never again will we require French Catholics to uphold selfish interests and policies of oppression in the name of Christ. They are aware that by combining initiative and fidelity, they have helped the Church to become more Christian. In the Resistance, and in the sufferings they endured afterwards, they rediscovered the value of that Renaissance canon which subsequent history had unfortunately obliterated: *Quidquid fit contra conscientiam aedificat ad gehennam.* "Everything that one does against his conscience strengthens the powers of hell." This is neither pride nor pretension: following one's conscience demands an effort of clearsightedness and knowledge; it requires modesty and a flexibility which those who blindly follow orders do not need.

The men of the Catholic avant-garde are representatives of the generation which emerged with the Resistance. Across these faces there passes a reflection of the Resurrection, for they have borne witness for these twenty years of history. Despite mistakes and discouragements, they look forward to the new world which is emerging; they know better than anyone that there can now be no turning back.

Notes

I Christianity and the Modern World

1 Henri de Lubac, S.J., *Catholicism: A Study of Dogma in Relation to the Corporate Destiny of Mankind* (New York: Mentor-Omega, 1964), pp. 176–178.

2 M. I. Montuclard, "L'Eglise et les valeurs modernes," in "La crise de la civilisation chrétienne," *Jeunesse de l'Eglise*, No. 5 (1944), pp. 12–17.

3 *Ibid.*, pp. 26–27.

4 R. P. Sertillanges, "Le christianisme a-t-il devirilisé l'homme?" in *Jeunesse de l'Eglise*, No. 2 (1943), p. 82.

5 Pierre Teilhard de Chardin, *The Phenomenon of Man* (New York: Harper & Brothers, 1959), pp. 283–285.

6 Pierre Teilhard de Chardin, *The Divine Milieu* (New York: Harper & Row, 1960), pp. 38–40.

7 Emmanuel Mounier, "L'agonie du christianisme," *Esprit* (May, 1946), pp. 726–727.

8 M. I. Montuclard, "L'Evangile captif," *Jeunesse de l'Eglise*, No. 10 (1949).

9 M. I. Montuclard, "L'Eglise et les valeurs modernes," *loc. cit.*

10 Yves Congar, *Vraie et fausse reforme dans l'Eglise* (Paris: ed. du Cerf, 1950), pp. 58–59.

11 André Depierre, "Témoignage," *Esprit* (August-September, 1946), pp. 321–344.

II A Mission Country

1 Maisie Ward, *France Pagan? The Mission of Abbé Godin* (New York: Sheed & Ward, 1949), pp. 96–98.

2 Emmanuel Cardinal Suhard, *Carnets spirituels* (Paris: ed. de la Bonne Press, 1952).

3 Henri Perrin, *Priest and Worker: The Autobiography of Henri Perrin* (New York: Holt, Rinehart and Winston, 1964), pp. 101–102.

4 Emmanuel Cardinal Suhard, *Priests Among Men* (Notre Dame, Ind.: Fides Press, 1951), pp. 39–41, 50.

5 *Ibid.*, p. 51.

6 P. Toulat, A. Bougeard, J. Templier, *Les chrétiens dans le monde rural* (Paris: ed. du Seuil, 1964), pp. 59–60, 319.
7 Henri Perrin, *op. cit.*, pp. 192–194.
8 *Ibid.*, pp. 210–212.
9 Jean Lacroix, "L'Eglise et la Mission," *Esprit* (December, 1953), pp. 711–715.
10 M. I. Montuclard, *Les evénements et la foi* (Paris: ed. du Seuil, 1951), pp. 55–56.
11 Jean Lacroix, *loc. cit.*
12 M. I. Montuclard, *op. cit.*, pp. 56–60, 62, 69–70, 71–72.
13 *The Worker-Priests, A Collective Documentation* (London: Routledge & Kegan Paul, 1956), pp. 196–202.
14 Emmanuel Cardinal Suhard, *Priests Among Men, op. cit.*, p. 49.
15 M. D. Chenu, O.P., "Le sacerdoce des prêtres-ouvriers," *La vie intellectuelle* (February, 1954), p. 175.
16 François Perroux, "Honneur des pionniers," *Esprit* (March, 1954), p. 409.

III   Toward a Christian Realism

1 *The Degrees of Knowledge*, trans. G. B. Phelan (New York: Charles Scribner's Sons, 1959).
2 Yves de Montcheuil, "L'idée de civilisation chrétienne," *L'Eglise et le monde actuel* (Paris: ed. Témoignage chrétien, 1945), pp. 33–34.
3 Barrère's address was published as part of the Proceedings of the 47th session of the ACJ National Council, *Positions* (Paris: ed. de l'Epi, 1956), pp. 53–55.
4 *Documentation catholique*, No. 1,237 (October 28, 1956), pp. 379 ff.
5 *Note doctrinale de l'ACA sur l'ACJF et les mouvements des jeunes*, October 1956 meeting (published by the study bureau of the Centre nationale d'études pastorales et pédagogiques, October 30, 1956), Communication 856.
6 Henri Marrou, "Du bon usage d'une encyclique," *Esprit* (February, 1965), pp. 562–570.
7 Dominique Dubarle, O.P., *Civilisation de l'atome* (Paris: ed. du Cerf, 1962), pp. 248–250.
8 Yves Congar, O.P., "Eglise et monde," *Esprit* (February, 1965), pp. 337 ff.
9 François Perroux, "Notre civilisation, est-elle malade?" in "Les Désordres de l'homme," *Semaine des intellectuels catholiques*, 1960 (Paris: ed. Pierre Horay, 1961), pp. 127–130.
10 Abbé Pierre [Goues], "Avant tout," *Faim et soif*, No. 56 (1964), pp. 9 ff.

IV The Church Apostolic

1 G. Michonneau, *Revolution in a City Parish* (London: Blackfriars, 1951), pp. 8–12.
2 G. Michonneau, *Pas de vie chrétienne sans communauté* (Paris: ed. du Cerf, 1960), p. 104.
3 M. D. Chenu, O.P., "Anthropologie et liturgie," *La Maison-Dieu*, No. 12 (1947), pp. 60–62.
4 M. A. Couturier, O.P., *Se garder libre, journal 1947–1954* (Paris: ed. du Cerf, 1961), pp. 102–103.
5 P. R. Régamey, O.P., *Religious Art in the Twentieth Century* (New York: Herder & Herder, 1963), pp. 109–112.
6 René Voillaume, *Lettres aux Fraternités* (Paris: ed. du Cerf, 1960), I, 273–275.
7 E. Roche, S.J., *La Nouvelle Revue théologique* (February, 1957), pp. 113–114.
8 *La Maison-Dieu*, No. 31, p. 10.
9 P. R. Régamey, O.P., et al., *Redécouverte du Jeune* (Paris: ed. du Cerf, 1959), pp. 434–436.
10 G. Morel, S.J., *Le sens de l'existence selon saint Jean de la Croix* (Paris: ed. Aubier, 1961), III, 156–158.
11 Robert de Montvalon, "L'Eglise de France en état de concile," *Chronique Sociale de France*, No. 3–4 (June 15, 1962), p. 117.

V The Secular City

1 Henri Marrou, "Schéma de réforme universitaire," *Esprit* (December, 1944), pp. 109–110.
2 Jacques Natanson, *Le Monde* (June 6, 1959).
3 Henri Marrou, "Polémique autour de l'école libre," *Esprit* (March, 1945), p. 528.
4 Emmanuel Mounier, "Christian Faith and Civilization," *Cross Currents* (Fall, 1950), pp. 18–19.
5 Joseph Vialatoux and André Latreille, "Christianity and Laicity," *Cross Currents* (Winter, 1952), pp. 17–20.
6 Joseph Hours, "L'expérience du MRP," *La vie intellectuelle* (May, 1948).
7 François Mauriac, *L'Express* (December 8, 1955).
8 *Ibid.* (December 22, 1955).
9 Abbé Boulier, "Les voies de l'initiative," *Esprit* (August-September, 1946).
10 Emmanuel Mounier, *Feu la chrétienté* (Paris: ed. du Seuil, 1951), pp. 11–12.

11 M. I. Montuclard, "Eglise et parti," in *Les chrétiens et la politique*, ed. Henri Guillemin (Paris: ed. du Temps Présent, 1948), pp. 162–165.

12 J. M. Domenach, "Conscience politique et conscience religieuse," *Esprit* (March, 1958), pp. 350–351.

13 *Ibid.*, pp. 356–358.

14 Henri Bartoli, "Les chrétiens vers une civilisation du travail," *Esprit* (July, 1952), pp. 20–25.

15 Henri Bartoli, "Conditionnement de la foi," *Esprit* (November, 1954), pp. 594–599.

16 André Mandouze, "Prendre la main tendue," in *Les chrétiens et la politique, op. cit.*, pp. 54–55, 62–63, 71–75.

17 A. J. Maydieu and A. Z. Serrand, "A propos des chrétiens progressistes," *La vie intellectuelle* (March, 1949), pp. 223–224.

18 Paul Fraisse, "De la liberté politique des catholiques," *Esprit* (May, 1952), pp. 882–883.

19 Directors of *La Quinzaine*, published in *La vie intellectuelle* (March, 1949), pp. 278–280.

20 Jean Lacroix, Response to an inquiry titled "Catholiques de droite, catholiques de gauche," *Chronique sociale de France* (December 30, 1956), pp. 637–638.

21 Statement of C. Savouillan, representing the *Reconstruction* group within the CFTC at the regional labor conference held at Puteaux in May 1953.

22 Fernand Boulard, *Problèmes missionaires de la France rurale* (Paris: ed. du Cerf, 1949), pp. 139–144.

23 P. Toulat, A. Bougeard, and J. Templier, *Les chrétiens dans le monde rural* (Paris: ed. du Seuil, 1964), pp. 59–61.

VI   The Struggle Against Colonialism

1 J. M. Domenach, *L'Affaire Henri Martin* (Paris: ed. Gallimard), pp. 246–247.

2 François Mauriac, "Bloc-Notes," *L'Express* (May 7, 1954).

3 Louis Massignon, *Esprit* (September, 1953), p. 385.

4 Pierre-Henri Simon, *Contre la torture* (Paris: ed. du Seuil, 1957), pp. 68–71.

VII   World Violence and World Peace

1 Robert de Montvalon, "Ces Pays qu'on n'appellera plus colonies," *Témoignage chrétien* (Paris: 1955), pp. 106–110.

2 Declaration of the French Bishops of West Africa and Togo, April 24, 1955. *Documentation catholique*, No. 1200 (May 29, 1955), col. 665.

3 L. J. Lebret, O.P., *Suicide ou survie de l'Occident?* (Paris: ed. Ouvrières, 1958), pp. 364–366.

4 H. Chappoulie, "Conférence à la quinzaine missionnaire de Lille," *Documentation catholique*, No. 1,215 (October 10, 1955), col. 1, pp. 373 ff.

5 P. R. Régamey, O.P., *Non-Violence and the Christian Conscience* (New York: Herder & Herder, 1966), pp. 66–70.

6 Emmanuel Mounier, "Les équivoques du pacifism," *Esprit* (February, 1949), pp. 186–189.

7 P. R. Régamey, O.P., *loc. cit.*

8 Jean Frisque, S.A.M., "Comment l'Eglise peut-elle rassembler les peuples différents?" *Terre entière*, No. 5 (1964), pp. 80–86.

9 P. A. Lesort, "Rencontre des religions et rencontre des personnes," *Bulletin du cercle saint Jean Baptiste*, No. 24 (1963), pp. 93–94.